Mastering Cybersecurity Ethics

Mastering Cybersecurity and Ethical Hacking: Defense and Offense in the Digital World

Julian Conrad

Table of Contents

INTRODUCTION

Cybersecurity has become a significant concern in a world that is becoming more digitally linked. Technology's explosive growth has given rise to previously unheard-of advantages and opportunities, but it has also made us vulnerable to increasing threats. The digital era offers a new playing field for attackers and defenders alike, with threats ranging from cyberattacks that threaten vital infrastructure to data breaches that expose private and financial information.

Amidst this landscape of challenges and vulnerabilities arises a powerful ally in the battle for digital security: ethical hacking. Known by many as "white hat hackers," ethical hackers use their strong technical abilities to strengthen and safeguard our online security. They act as protectors of the digital sphere, applying their expertise to find vulnerabilities before malicious hackers can take advantage of them. To fully comprehend and become an expert in this ever-evolving and vital topic, this e-book, "Mastering Cybersecurity Ethics: Mastering Cybersecurity and Ethical Hacking - Defense and Offense in the Digital World," is an excellent resource.

This e-book will provide you with the knowledge and resources you need to successfully navigate the complicated world of cybersecurity, whether you're an individual worried about your online privacy, a business owner trying to protect your company's assets, or an aspiring cybersecurity specialist. We will examine ethical hacking, delve into the foundations of cybersecurity, and present insights into offensive and defensive tactics to protect your online presence.

We will explore cybersecurity fundamentals in the following chapters, covering everything from the nuances of penetration testing and vulnerability assessment to incident response and disaster recovery's vital role. We'll also look at new developments in the industry and technology to help you remain ahead of the curve in a always changing digital landscape.

This e-book will be your reliable travel companion in cybersecurity, whether your goal is to strengthen the defenses around your company, further your career in the field, or learn more about securing yourself and your data online. By the time you turn the last page, we hope you will have a thorough understanding of cybersecurity and ethical hacking and the self-assurance to traverse the digital world with skill and resilience.

Together, let's take on this life-changing adventure as we examine the complex dance between offense and defense in the digital sphere to ensure you're ready for all the opportunities and problems that come with living in the digital age.

Welcome to "Mastering Cybersecurity Ethics: Mastering Cybersecurity and Ethical Hacking - Defense and Offense in the Digital World."

CHAPTER I

Understanding Cybersecurity

What is cybersecurity?

In today's hyper-connected world, "cybersecurity" has become a household name. It's a concept that transcends the boundaries of business, government, and individual life, touching every facet of our increasingly digital existence. Cybersecurity represents the collective effort to protect our digital systems, networks, and data from a barrage of ever-evolving threats. This section explores the multifaceted nature of cybersecurity, its fundamental principles, and its paramount importance in the modern age.

At its essence, cybersecurity is the practice of safeguarding digital assets against unauthorized access, damage, theft, or other forms of exploitation. These digital assets encompass a broad spectrum, ranging from personal information stored on our smartphones to the critical infrastructure that underpins a nation's economy. Cybersecurity is not just about thwarting hackers; it's about ensuring digital resources' confidentiality, integrity, and availability.

In cybersecurity, three primary objectives guide all efforts: confidentiality, integrity, and availability, often called the CIA triad. Confidentiality ensures that sensitive information remains private and accessible only to authorized individuals or entities. Integrity ensures that data remains unaltered and trustworthy, and availability ensures data and systems are accessible when needed.

To achieve these objectives, cybersecurity employs a multi-layered approach. First and foremost is the use of robust authentication mechanisms, like passwords, biometrics, and two-factor authentication, to confirm the identity of users and systems. Access controls further restrict who can access what, with varying privilege levels. Encryption protects data during transmission and storage, rendering it unreadable to unauthorized parties.

Firewalls and intrusion detection systems act as sentinels, monitoring network traffic for suspicious activities and blocking or alerting administrators to potential threats. Antivirus and anti-malware software serve as digital guardians, scanning for and eliminating malicious software that could compromise system integrity. Regular updates in software and patches are crucial to plugging vulnerabilities that hackers might exploit.

However, cybersecurity is not just a technical endeavor; it's also about fostering a culture of awareness and vigilance. Social engineering attacks, where hackers manipulate individuals into divulging sensitive information, are as prevalent as ever. Therefore, training and education play a pivotal role in strengthening cybersecurity. Employees and individuals must be aware of common threats like phishing, where fraudulent emails or messages attempt to deceive recipients into revealing confidential information.

Furthermore, the cybersecurity landscape is constantly changing. As technology advances, so do cybercriminals' strategies. New exploits are created, and new vulnerabilities surface. Consequently, cybersecurity experts need to be flexible and always learning new things. Proactive measures, such as proactive penetration testing and threat intelligence gathering, are necessary to stay ahead of the curve.

The importance of cybersecurity cannot be overstated. It transcends individual interests and extends to the well-being of organizations, governments, and society. A successful cyberattack can result in financial loss, reputational damage, and sometimes even threaten national security. As our reliance on digital systems deepens, the consequences of a breach become more severe.

In conclusion, cybersecurity is the defender of our digital environment, ensuring the availability, confidentiality, and integrity of our systems and data. It's a dynamic, constantly changing sector that calls for both a cultural shift toward greater awareness and responsibility as well as technological proficiency. Strong cybersecurity safeguards are crucial in a world where technology is becoming more and more integrated into our daily lives. The shield protects our linked world's trust and security by putting up a barrier against the innumerable risks that lurk in the digital shadows.

Historical context and evolution of cybersecurity

The evolution of cybersecurity is a fascinating journey through time, reflecting the rapid transformation of our digital landscape and the ever-escalating battle between those who seek to exploit vulnerabilities and those who endeavor to protect against them. To understand the modern concept of cybersecurity, it's crucial to trace its historical context, from its humble beginnings to its current state as an indispensable element of our interconnected world.

When computing first began, a "computer" was more like a room-sized machine than the modern, sleek devices we carry in our pockets. This is where the history of cybersecurity begins. Computers were mostly employed in science and the military in the 1940s and 1950s. Because these early computers were isolated and had little use, security concerns during this era were quite low.

However, the 1960s witnessed the dawn of networking and the birth of the internet. As computers became interconnected, the need for security mechanisms became apparent. One of the first notable events in the history of cybersecurity was the development of the Compatible Time-Sharing System (CTSS) at the Massachusetts Institute of Technology (MIT) in 1961. This system introduced the concept of user accounts and passwords, laying the foundation for authentication and access control—a fundamental aspect of modern cybersecurity.

The 1970s marked a significant milestone with the introduction of the first computer virus. The "Creeper" virus, designed by Bob Thomas at BBN Technologies, was benign by today's standards, but it demonstrated the potential for malicious code to propagate through computer networks. In response, the first antivirus software, "Reaper," was created to remove the Creeper virus, marking the birth of the ongoing battle between malware creators and cybersecurity defenders.

The 1980s brought about a proliferation of personal computers, making computing more accessible to individuals. However, this accessibility also opened the door to new security threats. The "Morris Worm" of 1988, created by Robert Tappan Morris, infected thousands of computers and became one of the first instances of a major cyberattack. This event prompted increased awareness of the need for cybersecurity measures.

The 1990s witnessed the widespread adoption of the internet, revolutionizing communication and commerce. With this growth came a surge in cybercrime, including hacking, viruses, and identity theft. The field of cybersecurity expanded to encompass not only technical aspects but also legal and regulatory considerations. In 1999, the U.S. government established the National Infrastructure Protection Center (NIPC), a precursor to today's cybersecurity agencies, emphasizing the importance of protecting critical infrastructure from digital threats.

The 21st century brought cybersecurity to the forefront of global concerns. High-profile breaches, such as the 2007 cyberattack on Estonia and the 2010 Stuxnet worm that targeted Iran's nuclear facilities, demonstrated the real-world impact of cyber threats. Governments, businesses, and individuals recognized the need for robust cybersecurity measures.

Cybersecurity is a vast and multifaceted field encompassing a wide range of technologies and practices. It includes using advanced encryption, intrusion detection systems, and artificial intelligence to protect against threats. Ethical hacking and penetration testing have become essential tools for identifying vulnerabilities before malicious actors can exploit them.

In conclusion, the evolution and historical background of cybersecurity highlight its critical importance in our increasingly digital world. From the earliest days of computing to the current complex environment, cybersecurity has developed and changed to meet ever changing threats. As our reliance on technology grows, the history of cybersecurity shows how human creativity can persevere in the face of technological difficulties, serving as a constant reminder that the fight to safeguard our digital future is crucial and continuous.

Key cybersecurity threats and challenges

The rapid growth of technology in the modern era has changed our way of living, working, and interacting with one another. All facets of our globally interconnected world are affected by cybersecurity risks and difficulties that have emerged as a result of the digital revolution. In their efforts to safeguard sensitive data and vital infrastructure from malevolent actors, individuals, organizations, and governments must all be aware of these risks.

Malware, a general word for malicious software intended to infiltrate, damage, or steal data from computer systems, is one of the most common cybersecurity concerns. Malware can take many different forms, such as Trojan, worms, viruses, ransomware, and spyware. These attacks frequently leverage social engineering techniques or software weaknesses to trick users into downloading or running them. Malware can cause chaos by encrypting data, obtaining control of a device, or exfiltrating information once it has entered a system.

Another well-known cybersecurity issue that is fueled by social engineering techniques is phishing. Attacks using phishing techniques involve fraudulent emails, texts, or websites that mimic reputable organizations like banks, governments, or well-known businesses. Through these dishonest communications, consumers are tricked into disclosing private information like credit card numbers, passwords, or personal information. Because phishing assaults are more sophisticated, it is more difficult to recognize and defend against them.

Attacks using ransomware have become more well-known recently as a particularly harmful type of malware. Cybercriminals encrypt a victim's data in a ransomware attack, making it unreadable. Next, a ransom demand is presented to the victim in return for the decryption key. Since it encourages criminal behavior and does not ensure the safe return of data, paying the ransom is dangerous and frequently discouraged. In order to lessen the effects of ransomware attacks, organizations are advised to implement strong backup and recovery procedures.

Critical infrastructure cyberattacks are becoming a serious threat. Transportation networks, water treatment facilities, and power grids are especially susceptible to cyberattacks because of their growing reliance on digital technologies. A successful attack on vital infrastructure might have disastrous repercussions, including posing a threat to public safety or causing service interruptions. To protect national interests, governments and organizations need to give the security of these systems first priority. The

issues associated with cybersecurity have taken on a new dimension due to the Internet of Things. IoT gadgets with weak security measures, such as cameras, smart thermostats, and home automation systems, are frequently linked to the internet. Because of this, IoT devices are vulnerable to hacking, which gives hackers the opportunity to use them as gateways into larger networks. The need for better security standards and practices is highlighted by the increasing number of IoT devices.

The proliferation of cloud computing has brought about unique cybersecurity challenges. Storing sensitive data and applications in the cloud can be convenient but requires a shared responsibility model between cloud providers and users. Misconfigured cloud settings, inadequate access controls, or weak encryption can expose data to unauthorized access or data breaches. Organizations must diligently assess and monitor their cloud security posture.

Emerging technologies in cybersecurity, such quantum computing and artificial intelligence (AI), present both potential and risks. AI can enhance threat detection and response, but attackers can also harness it to automate and scale their attacks. Quantum computing, when fully realized, could break widely used encryption methods, necessitating the development of quantum-resistant cryptographic solutions.

In conclusion, cybersecurity threats and challenges are dynamic and ever-evolving, reflecting the relentless innovation of cybercriminals and the expanding attack surface of our digital world. Addressing these threats requires a multifaceted approach, encompassing robust technical defenses, user awareness and education, and proactive threat intelligence. As technology advances, cybersecurity must remain a top priority for individuals, organizations, and governments to ensure the security and resilience of our interconnected society.

CHAPTER II

The Fundamentals of Ethical Hacking

What is ethical hacking?

In an increasingly digitized world where our lives are intertwined with technology, the term "hacker" often carries a negative connotation. It conjures images of cybercriminals orchestrating malicious attacks, breaching systems, and compromising sensitive data. However, there is a different kind of hacker – the ethical hacker, also known as a "white hat hacker." Ethical hacking represents a fundamental component of cybersecurity, where individuals and professionals use their hacking skills not for malicious purposes but to safeguard digital systems and networks from cyber threats.

Ethical hacking, sometimes called penetration testing or white-hat hacking, involves authorized attempts to exploit vulnerabilities within computer systems, networks, or applications. These authorized attempts are conducted with the explicit consent of the system's owner or organization, distinguishing ethical hackers from malicious hackers who operate without permission. Ethical hacking aims to identify and rectify vulnerabilities before malicious actors can exploit them, ultimately enhancing the security of the target system.

Ethical hackers employ various techniques and methodologies to simulate potential cyberattacks. They examine the target system's architecture, configuration, and code, searching for weaknesses that adversaries could exploit. Everyday activities performed by ethical hackers include vulnerability scanning, penetration testing, and social engineering assessments.

One of the primary activities of ethical hacking is vulnerability assessment. This process involves systematically scanning a system or network for known vulnerabilities. Ethical hackers use specialized software tools to identify weak points in software, hardware, or configurations that attackers could exploit. Once vulnerabilities are identified, ethical hackers collaborate with the system owner to prioritize and address these issues.

Penetration testing is another essential aspect of ethical hacking. It goes beyond vulnerability scanning by actively attempting to exploit identified weaknesses. Ethical hackers seek to mimic the tactics and techniques used by malicious hackers but intend to assess the system's resilience and discover potential entry points. By successfully penetrating a system, ethical hackers provide valuable insights into the organization's security posture and highlight areas that require immediate attention.

Social engineering assessments are yet another dimension of ethical hacking. Ethical hackers employ psychological manipulation techniques in these assessments to test an organization's human-centric security vulnerabilities. This can involve phishing attacks, where hackers craft convincing emails to trick employees into revealing sensitive information or clicking on malicious links. By evaluating an organization's susceptibility to social engineering tactics, ethical hackers help improve employee awareness and training.

Ethical hacking has changed dramatically over time, keeping up with the constantly shifting cybersecurity environment. For ethical hackers to stay up to date with new technology and emerging threats, they must constantly refresh their knowledge and abilities. Certification programs like Certified Ethical Hacker (CEH) and Offensive Security Certified Professional (OSCP) provide formal training and recognition for ethical hackers, helping them stay current in their field.

Ethical hacking plays a critical role in modern cybersecurity. It is a proactive defense mechanism, enabling organizations to identify and rectify vulnerabilities before malicious actors exploit them. By engaging ethical hackers, organizations demonstrate a commitment to cybersecurity, data protection, and the privacy of their customers and stakeholders. In an era where cyber threats are pervasive and ever-evolving, ethical hacking is a practice and a philosophy that underscores the importance of securing the digital world for the benefit of all.

Ethical hacking vs. malicious hacking

In the intricate realm of hacking, a profound moral divide shapes the intentions and actions of individuals who delve into the intricacies of computer systems and networks. On one side, we find ethical hackers, often referred to as "white hat hackers," and on the other, malicious hackers, commonly known as "black hat hackers." These two distinct categories represent opposing forces in the digital landscape, with divergent motivations, methodologies, and consequences. Understanding the fundamental differences between ethical and malicious hacking is essential in navigating the complex world of cybersecurity.

In order to find flaws and vulnerabilities, ethical hackers willfully probe computer networks, systems, and applications with the owners' explicit consent. Ethical hacking objective is to enhance the security and resilience of the systems they target by simulating hypothetical intrusions using their knowledge, abilities, and resources. They are driven by a sense of responsibility and a commitment to protect data, privacy, and critical infrastructure. Ethical hackers follow strict codes of conduct and adhere to legal and ethical guidelines, ensuring that their actions are transparent, authorized, and focused on strengthening the defenses of the digital world.

In stark contrast, malicious hacking embodies actions taken with ill intent, often driven by personal gain, mischief, or malice. Black hat hackers engage in unauthorized activities aimed at exploiting vulnerabilities, breaching systems, and causing harm to individuals, organizations, or even nations. Their actions may include stealing sensitive data, conducting financial fraud, launching distributed denial-of-service (DDoS) attacks, or disseminating malware for personal or criminal gain. The motivations of malicious hackers are as varied as their actions, but they invariably lack the ethical foundation that guides their white hat counterparts.

A key distinguishing factor between ethical hacking and malicious hacking lies in the concept of consent. Ethical hackers operate with explicit authorization from system owners or organizations, conducting their activities within agreed-upon boundaries. Malicious hackers, conversely, trespass into systems without permission, violating the law and ethical standards. This fundamental difference underscores the ethical and legal boundaries that separate these two groups.

Ethical hackers follow a structured and documented approach to their work. They engage in vulnerability assessment and penetration testing to uncover weaknesses, report their findings, and collaborate with system owners to rectify the identified vulnerabilities. The ethical hacker's ultimate goal is to enhance security, prevent data breaches, and fortify the digital landscape against cyber threats. Their work contributes to the development of robust cybersecurity practices and the protection of sensitive information.

In contrast, malicious hackers rely on covert tactics and stealthy maneuvers to evade detection and exploit vulnerabilities for personal gain or disruption. They often employ various deception techniques, such as social engineering, to manipulate individuals into revealing sensitive information. Their actions are driven by self-interest and often have detrimental consequences for victims, ranging from financial losses to reputational damage and emotional distress.

Malicious hacking and ethical hacking are separated by ethics and legality. Malicious hacking is now a crime in many nations as a result of laws and regulations that specifically make it illegal to gain unauthorized access to computer systems and networks. Ethical hackers, by contrast, operate within the framework of legal and ethical boundaries, ensuring their actions remain lawful and transparent.

In conclusion, the chasm between ethical hacking and malicious hacking is a moral and ethical one, reflecting the profound impact that individual choices can have in the digital age. Ethical hackers are cybersecurity guardians, using their skills for the greater good by protecting systems and data from threats. In contrast, malicious hackers sow discord and chaos, driven by personal gain or destructive intent. Understanding this dichotomy is essential in appreciating the importance of ethical hacking as a crucial component in safeguarding our interconnected world and preserving the trust and integrity of the digital realm.

The role of ethical hackers in cybersecurity

These days, with cyber threats constantly attacking the digital world, ethical hackers, sometimes known as "white hat hackers," play a crucial role in defending against these ever-evolving and persistent enemies. In cybersecurity, ethical hackers are essential because their knowledge and techniques are used to safeguard networks, computer systems, and private information. This section examines the various ways ethical hackers protect the digital sphere, their working methods, and the wider ramifications of their efforts in a world growing more interconnected every day.

At its core, the role of ethical hackers is to mimic the tactics and techniques employed by malicious hackers, but with a crucial distinction—ethical hackers operate with explicit authorization and follow a strict code of conduct. Their mission is not to exploit vulnerabilities but to proactively identify, assess, and mitigate them. They assist organizations and individuals in fortifying their defenses, ultimately enhancing the overall cybersecurity posture.

Vulnerability assessment is one of the primary tasks performed by ethical hackers. They meticulously scan systems, networks, and applications for known vulnerabilities, weaknesses, or misconfigurations. Employing specialized software tools, ethical hackers identify potential entry points for cybercriminals, ensuring that these vulnerabilities are promptly addressed. By conducting vulnerability assessments, they provide valuable insights into the target system's security posture, enabling organizations to take proactive measures to mitigate risks.

Penetration testing is another critical aspect of the ethical hacker's role. Unlike vulnerability assessment, penetration testing goes a step further by actively attempting to exploit identified vulnerabilities. Ethical hackers simulate cyberattacks to evaluate how systems and networks respond to real-world threats. The insights gained from penetration testing enable organizations to understand their vulnerabilities' actual impact and prioritize remediation efforts effectively.

Ethical hackers also engage in social engineering assessments, focusing on the human element of cybersecurity. They employ psychological manipulation techniques to test an organization's susceptibility to social engineering tactics, such as phishing attacks. By simulating these scenarios, ethical hackers help organizations identify potential weaknesses in employee awareness and training, ultimately strengthening the human layer of cybersecurity defenses.

One of the critical methodologies ethical hackers employ is responsible disclosure. Ethical hackers responsibly disclose their findings to the affected organization or system owner when they discover vulnerabilities. This practice ensures that the vulnerabilities are addressed promptly and transparently, preventing malicious hackers from exploiting them. Responsible disclosure promotes a collaborative approach to cybersecurity, emphasizing cooperation between ethical hackers and system owners in the mutual interest of safeguarding digital assets.

The role of ethical hackers extends beyond simply identifying and mitigating vulnerabilities. They actively contribute to the development of robust cybersecurity practices and strategies. Ethical hackers often work closely with organizations to provide recommendations, guidance, and best practices to enhance overall security. Their expertise helps organizations make informed decisions regarding security investments and measures, ensuring that resources are allocated effectively to protect against emerging threats.

Ethical hackers also serve as educators, raising awareness about cybersecurity among individuals, businesses, and government agencies. Their knowledge and experience are invaluable in disseminating information about the latest threats and preventive measures. Ethical hackers empower individuals and organizations to become more resilient in the face of cyber threats by sharing their insights through training programs, workshops, and public awareness campaigns.

In conclusion, the role of ethical hackers in cybersecurity is one of vigilance, responsibility, and dedication to the greater good. They operate on the frontlines of the digital battlefield, using their skills and expertise to protect against cyber threats. Ethical hackers are not just defenders of systems and data but champions of transparency, collaboration, and the shared mission to secure our interconnected world. In an age where the digital realm is inseparable from our daily lives, the role of ethical hackers stands as a beacon of trust and resilience in the face of relentless cyber adversaries.

CHAPTER III

Cybersecurity Frameworks and Standards

Overview of cybersecurity frameworks (NIST, ISO 27001, CIS)

In the dynamic realm of cybersecurity, organizations are faced with a challenging task: creating and implementing effective strategies to safeguard their digital assets against potential attacks. Thankfully, cybersecurity frameworks offer essential guidance and tools to support enterprises in strengthening their security postures. Comprehensive methods to cybersecurity are provided by three well-known cybersecurity frameworks: the Center for Internet Security (CIS) Controls, ISO/IEC 27001, and the NIST or the National Institute of Standards and Technology Cybersecurity Framework. An overview of these frameworks is given in this section, along with an emphasis on their key features and importance in improving cybersecurity procedures.

The National Institute of Standards and Technology of U.S. created the well-known and significant NIST Cybersecurity Framework. Executive Order 13636, which mandated the creation of a voluntary framework to enhance critical infrastructure cybersecurity, prompted the creation of this system. The NIST Framework offers enterprises a methodical way to control and minimize cybersecurity risk.

The NIST 5 Functions—Identify, Protect, Detect, Respond, and Recover—are the foundational elements of the system. Every function has a number of categories and subcategories that help firms evaluate their cybersecurity posture and create security-enhancing plans. The Protect function takes care of protecting vital assets, whilst the Identify function concentrates on comprehending and addressing cybersecurity concerns. While the Respond function handles incident response, the Recover function concentrates on restoring services and lessening the impact of cybersecurity incidents. The Detect function places an emphasis on continuous monitoring for cybersecurity events.

The adaptability of the NIST Framework, which makes it useful for businesses of all sizes and sectors, is one of its advantages. It encourages a risk-based strategy, which enables businesses to customize their cybersecurity initiatives to meet their particular requirements and risk profiles. In addition, the NIST Framework promotes collaboration as well as communication between technical and business teams, which supports a proactive and all-encompassing approach to cybersecurity.

The International Organization for Standardization (or ISO) along with the International Electrotechnical Commission (or IEC) produced ISO/IEC 27001 as an international standard for information security management systems (ISMS). This framework offers a methodical approach to sensitive information management and security.

A set of requirements that specify the needs for creating, putting into practice, maintaining, and continuously enhancing an ISMS form the foundation of ISO/IEC 27001 standards. These standards, which cover risk assessment, risk treatment, security policy development, and continuous monitoring and improvement, must be followed by organizations applying for certification. The framework places a strong emphasis on the necessity of an all-encompassing risk management procedure in order to properly recognize, evaluate, and address information security threats.

The focus placed by ISO/IEC 27001 on formalizing and documenting security procedures is one of its standout characteristics. Security policies, risk assessments, and control procedures are just a few of the documentation that organizations seeking certification must produce and keep up to date. Being globally recognized and signifying an organization's dedication to information security, ISO/IEC 27001 certification is a significant credential for companies looking to gain the trust of their partners and clients.

A nonprofit group created the Center for Internet Security (CIS) Controls, a collection of cybersecurity best practices. These controls offer a methodical and prioritized way to improve the cybersecurity posture of a business. Because the CIS Controls are divided into three implementation groups, companies with different degrees of security maturity can use them.

The CIS Controls encompass 20 specific security controls that cover various aspects of cybersecurity, including asset management, continuous vulnerability assessment, data protection, and incident response. These controls are designed to be actionable and provide clear guidance for organizations to improve their security. The CIS Controls also emphasize the importance of continuous monitoring and assessment to adapt to evolving threats.

One of the strengths of the CIS Controls is their practicality and adaptability. They offer organizations a roadmap for implementing effective security measures, starting with fundamental controls and progressing to more advanced ones as their cybersecurity maturity grows. The CIS Controls are frequently updated to address emerging threats, ensuring organizations stay ahead of evolving cybersecurity challenges.

In conclusion, cybersecurity frameworks like the NIST Cybersecurity Framework, ISO/IEC 27001, and CIS Controls are invaluable resources for organizations seeking to enhance their cybersecurity postures. These frameworks provide structured approaches to identify and mitigate cybersecurity risks, fostering a proactive and strategic approach to security. While each framework has unique features and strengths, they all share a common goal: helping organizations protect their digital assets and sensitive information in an increasingly interconnected and threat-filled digital landscape.

Compliance and regulations in cybersecurity

The importance of cybersecurity cannot be emphasized in the constantly changing digital landscape of the twenty-first century, where data travels constantly across borders and industries. Regulations and compliance stand as strong foundations in this environment, offering the structure and direction that are vital to guarantee the protection and privacy of sensitive data. These rules are not just governmental red tape; rather, they are vital instruments that help people, businesses, and governments negotiate the dangerous seas of online threats and vulnerabilities.

Cybersecurity compliance and regulations encompass a broad spectrum of rules, standards, and guidelines established by various entities, including governments, industry bodies, and international organizations. These frameworks serve as blueprints for organizations, offering a structured path to effectively protect digital assets and mitigate risks. Their significance is manifold.

These regulations are, first and foremost, guardians of data protection. Strict safeguards are required to protect sensitive and personal data, such as those mandated by Health Insurance Portability and Accountability Act (or HIPAA) in the US and the General Data Protection Regulation (or GDPR) in Europe. Organizations that abide by these rules safeguard the integrity and confidentiality of data, defending people's right to privacy in a time when cybercrime and data breaches are commonplace.

Furthermore, compliance frameworks are powerful tools for risk management. They enable organizations to identify, assess, and manage cybersecurity risks systematically. By adhering to established standards, organizations can develop robust risk management strategies that help minimize the potential impact of security incidents. In an ever-changing cyber threat landscape, these frameworks provide a steady compass to navigate the treacherous terrain.

Standardization is another key facet of compliance and regulations. These frameworks establish common cybersecurity standards, ensuring consistent security across industries and sectors. This standardization simplifies risk assessment, auditing, and the sharing of best practices. Organizations of any size or industry can use these guidelines as a starting point for their security protocols, encouraging a unified and cooperative approach to cybersecurity.

In addition to setting the stage for proactive cybersecurity measures, compliance frameworks emphasize the importance of incident response. Many regulations require organizations to have well-defined incident response plans, ensuring they can swiftly and effectively respond to cybersecurity breaches. These plans help contain incidents and enable organizations to recover from them while minimizing damage to their reputation and operations.

The impact of compliance and regulations in cybersecurity extends far beyond individual organizations. They play a pivotal role in shaping the cybersecurity landscape of entire sectors and industries. For instance, the healthcare sector relies heavily on regulations like HIPAA to protect patient information, ensuring the confidentiality and integrity of medical records. Strict guidelines such as the Payment Card Industry Data Security Standard, abbreviated PCI DSS, are implemented in the financial sector to protect consumer information and financial activities.

Moreover, governments worldwide establish regulations to protect critical infrastructure and national security interests. Compliance frameworks like the NIST SP 800-53 and the Cybersecurity Maturity Model Certification (CMMC) guide government agencies and contractors in ensuring the reliability and security of essential services, resources, and information.

These compliance and regulatory measures significantly affect individual privacy, consumer trust, global commerce, and national security. They provide individuals with a shield for their personal data, safeguarding them from misuse and data breaches. Consumer trust in organizations is bolstered when compliance demonstrates a commitment to data security, fostering a more secure digital environment.

International organizations and multinational corporations in global commerce rely on compliance to navigate the complexities of data protection regulations across borders. Compliance ensures seamless international business operations while adhering to the diverse cybersecurity standards of different regions and countries.

National security is another critical aspect of compliance and regulations. Cybersecurity regulations protect critical infrastructure, safeguarding essential services and resources that a nation relies upon. Ensuring the security of these critical assets is paramount for maintaining the stability and resilience of a nation in an increasingly interconnected world.

Innovation is yet another indirect consequence of compliance and regulations in cybersecurity. As organizations strive to meet regulatory requirements, they invest in research and development to develop innovative cybersecurity technologies and practices. This innovation benefits not only the organizations themselves but also the broader cybersecurity community.

In conclusion, cybersecurity compliance and regulations are essential in securing the digital world. They are not constraints but guideposts that help organizations and individuals navigate the complex and dynamic landscape of cyber threats and vulnerabilities. While they pose challenges and costs, their benefits, including enhanced security, consumer trust, and a safer digital environment, are invaluable. In an age where data breaches and cyberattacks are prevalent, compliance and regulations stand as crucial guardians, preserving the security and privacy of digital assets for the advantage of individuals, organizations, and nations.

Implementing cybersecurity best practices

In an age where our lives are intricately entwined with technology, the importance of cybersecurity cannot be overstated. From personal information to critical infrastructure, the digital realm is rife with valuable assets that must be protected from the ever-evolving landscape of cyber threats. Implementing cybersecurity best practices is not just an option but a necessity to ensure the security and privacy of individuals, organizations, and governments alike. This section delves into cybersecurity, exploring the significance of best practices, fundamental principles, and practical steps to fortify defenses against cyber adversaries.

Cybersecurity best practices are guidelines, techniques, and strategies that have emerged through years of experience and lessons learned in the battle against cyber threats. They encapsulate the collective wisdom of cybersecurity experts and serve as a roadmap for individuals and organizations seeking to protect digital assets and sensitive information.

the scope and diversity of cyberthreats is among the strongest arguments for the idea of putting cybersecurity best practices into practice. Ransomware, phishing, malware, and advanced persistent threats are just a few of the persistent and ever-evolving strategies employed by cybercriminals. Best practices for cybersecurity offer an organized method for spotting and thwarting these attacks, assisting companies in maintaining a competitive edge in the never-ending cybersecurity race.

Considerable weight is also placed on the possible repercussions of a cyberattack. Financial losses, harm to one's reputation, legal ramifications, and concerns to national security can all arise from data breaches.

Adhering to best practices can help organizations drastically lower the risk and consequence of security breaches. Furthermore, in an increasingly connected world, individuals can also benefit from cybersecurity best practices to safeguard their privacy and personal information. These practices are not just for organizations, though.

Risk assessment, defense-in-depth, continuous monitoring, patch management, and personnel training are the cornerstones of cybersecurity best practices. The basis for risk assessment is knowledge of particular risks and vulnerabilities. The goal of defense-in-depth is to thwart different attack vectors by implementing numerous layers of security. Continuous monitoring guarantees that threats are identified and dealt with quickly. Patch management updates systems and software to fix vulnerabilities that are known to exist. Programs for employee awareness and training lessen the human element in security breaches.

Practical steps for implementing cybersecurity best practices include strong access controls, data encryption, incident response plans, regular backups, security updates, security awareness, and third-party assessments. These steps collectively contribute to a robust cybersecurity posture that can withstand the dynamic and evolving cyber threat landscape.

In conclusion, implementing cybersecurity best practices is not just a recommendation but an imperative. Cyber threats are omnipresent and ever-evolving, making it crucial for individuals and organizations to fortify their digital defenses. By adhering to fundamental principles and practical steps, we can collectively navigate the complex digital landscape more resiliently, safeguarding our digital assets and privacy in an interconnected world.

Cybersecurity is not a destination but an ongoing journey, and best practices are the compass that keeps us on the right path.

CHAPTER IV

Cyber Threat Intelligence

What is cyber threat intelligence?

In an era where the digital realm permeates every facet of our lives, "cybersecurity" has become synonymous with safeguarding our interconnected world. At the heart of this cybersecurity landscape lies a powerful concept: cyber threat intelligence (CTI). CTI represents the knowledge, data, and insights that empower individuals, organizations, and governments to understand, anticipate, and mitigate cyber threats. It is the cornerstone of modern cybersecurity, a proactive approach to countering the ever-evolving tactics and strategies employed by cybercriminals, hacktivists, nation-states, and other malicious actors.

Cyber threat intelligence is not a singular entity but a multifaceted process that begins with data collection. It encompasses many sources, from open-source information found in public forums and news articles to closed-source intelligence that includes proprietary data and insights. Technical sources, such as logs, network traffic data, and malware samples, are also pivotal in gathering information. This diverse data pool forms the foundation upon which CTI analysts work their magic.

The core of cyber threat intelligence lies in its analysis. Here, experts dissect the collected data to discern patterns, trends, and potential threats. They delve into the intricacies of malware, scrutinize the methods and vectors of attacks, and assess vulnerabilities in software and systems. This analytical process paints a comprehensive picture of the threat landscape, illuminating threat actors' modi operandi and motivations.

However, the journey continues after analysis; dissemination is equally crucial. Sharing cyber threat intelligence within and among organizations and with trusted partners and government agencies forms a collective defense against threats. Information sharing platforms like Information Sharing and Analysis Centers (ISACs) and industry-specific Information Sharing and Analysis Organizations (ISAOs) facilitate this exchange, bolstering the community's ability to respond to emerging threats swiftly.

The practical applications of cyber threat intelligence are far-reaching. It is a proactive tool for preventing cyberattacks by enabling organizations to shore up vulnerabilities and fortify defenses. It plays a critical role in detection, providing the means to identify unusual behavior, indicators of compromise, and emerging attack vectors. Moreover, when an attack does occur, CTI guides the incident response process, aiding in containment, eradication, and recovery efforts.

Attribution, another facet of CTI, helps identify the perpetrators of cyberattacks. This attribution is pivotal for diplomatic, legal, and strategic responses to cyber incidents. Additionally, cyber threat intelligence contributes to effective risk management, allowing organizations to strategically assess and prioritize cybersecurity risks.

In conclusion, cyber threat intelligence is the cornerstone of modern cybersecurity, providing the knowledge and insight needed to protect our digital world. Its proactive nature empowers organizations and individuals to effectively understand, anticipate, and counter cyber threats. Cyber threat intelligence is still crucial to protecting our globalized society from the ever-improving efforts of cybercriminals as the digital landscape changes.

Gathering and analyzing threat intelligence

In the modern digital landscape, where cyber threats evolve at an unprecedented pace, gathering and analyzing threat intelligence has become a critical skill. Threat intelligence is the knowledge and insights about cyber threats, vulnerabilities, and tactics malicious actors employ to compromise digital assets. This section explores the essential processes of gathering and analyzing threat intelligence, their significance in bolstering cybersecurity, and the strategies used to stay one step ahead of cyber adversaries.

Cyber threats are dynamic and relentless, posing substantial risks to organizations, governments, and individuals. To effectively defend against these threats, staying informed about the ever-evolving threat landscape is essential. This is where threat intelligence comes into play. Gathering and analyzing threat intelligence is not merely a proactive measure but a necessity for mitigating risks and ensuring the security of digital assets.

Threat intelligence serves several crucial purposes:

Identification of Threats: Threat intelligence provides real-time insights into emerging threats, allowing organizations to identify and understand the nature of potential attacks. This early identification is pivotal for proactive defense.

Understanding Tactics: Analyzing threat intelligence helps comprehend the tactics, techniques, and procedures (TTPs) employed by threat actors. This knowledge is instrumental in designing effective countermeasures.

Strategic Planning: Threat intelligence informs strategic planning by helping organizations assess the risks they face, allocate resources efficiently, and prioritize security measures based on threat level.

Incident Response: In a cyber incident, threat intelligence guides incident response efforts. It enables organizations to tailor their responses to the specific threat and mitigate the impact swiftly.

Gathering threat intelligence involves collecting data from a variety of sources. These sources include open-source intelligence (OSINT), which monitors publicly accessible information such as news articles, social media, and forums. Closed-source intelligence includes proprietary data sources, while technical sources encompass logs, network traffic data, and malware samples.

The collection process is an ongoing effort that systematically aggregates data from these sources. Automation plays a significant role in efficiently collecting and aggregating vast amounts of data. Threat intelligence feeds and platforms are used to continuously collect data, ensuring organizations stay current with the threat landscape.

Analyzing threat intelligence is the heart of the process. Experts dissect the collected data during this phase to identify patterns, trends, and potential threats. They scrutinize the tactics, techniques, and procedures used by threat actors to understand their modi operandi better.

This analysis includes dissecting malware, studying attack vectors, and assessing vulnerabilities in software and systems. Analysts also assess the credibility and relevance of the intelligence to determine its potential impact on the organization's security posture.

Machine learning and also artificial intelligence (or AI) have become valuable tools in analyzing threat intelligence. These technologies can rapidly process and correlate large volumes of data, helping analysts identify emerging threats and patterns that might go unnoticed through manual analysis alone.

Cyber adversaries are persistent and agile. Organizations should adopt a proactive technique to threat intelligence to stay ahead of them. This involves analyzing historical data and anticipating future threats based on current trends and intelligence. Collaboration and information sharing with other organizations, industry groups, and government agencies also play a crucial role in staying ahead of cyber adversaries.

Furthermore, threat intelligence should be incorporated into an organization's security strategy and decision-making processes. It should inform the deployment of security tools, the allocation of resources for threat mitigation, and the development of incident response plans. Organizations should constantly assess the effectiveness of their threat intelligence programs and adapt them to evolving threats.

In conclusion, gathering and analyzing threat intelligence is a cornerstone of modern cybersecurity. It empowers organizations to effectively understand, anticipate, and defend against cyber threats. Organizations can enhance their cybersecurity posture and mitigate risks by identifying threats, understanding tactics, and strategic planning. In a digital landscape where the only constant is change, threat intelligence is vital in safeguarding digital assets and ensuring the security and resilience of organizations and individuals in an interconnected world.

Applying threat intelligence for defense

The significance of cybersecurity in today's more digitally linked and networked society cannot be emphasized. As organizations and individuals rely more on digital systems and networks, the threat landscape has evolved, becoming more sophisticated and dangerous. To effectively defend against these cyber threats, organizations must adopt a proactive and strategic approach, and one of the key elements in this strategy is the application of cyber threat intelligence.

Cyber threat intelligence (CTI) refers to the information and insights gathered about potential cyber threats and adversaries. It encompasses data on emerging threats, vulnerabilities, attacker tactics, techniques, and procedures (TTPs), and can provide organizations with a deeper understanding of the evolving threat landscape. The application of CTI is crucial for organizations looking to bolster their defenses, and it can be approached in several ways.

Firstly, CTI assists in threat detection and prevention. Organizations can stay ahead of potential threats by continuously monitoring various sources, including dark web forums, malware repositories, and open-source intelligence feeds. CTI allows organizations to identify and understand emerging threats, enabling them to implement preventive measures before they become critical. For example, if a specific type of malware or attack method is identified through CTI, organizations can update their security systems to detect and block that threat.

Secondly, CTI enhances incident response capabilities. In the event of a cyberattack, time is of the essence. The quicker an organization can respond, the less damage is likely to occur. CTI can provide valuable information about attackers' tactics and tools, enabling security teams to respond effectively. This includes identifying indicators of compromise (IoCs), which can be used to hunt for signs of an ongoing breach and eradicate it promptly.

Moreover, CTI aids in attribution and understanding the motives behind cyberattacks. It can help organizations determine the source of the threat, whether it's a nation-state actor, cybercriminal gang, or hacktivist group. This information is crucial not only for responding to the immediate threat but also for determining the appropriate legal and diplomatic actions that may be necessary.

Additionally, CTI facilitates strategic decision-making in cybersecurity. It allows organizations to assess their vulnerabilities and weaknesses compared to the evolving threat landscape. Armed with this knowledge, they can allocate resources effectively to address their most critical security gaps. CTI also aids in making informed decisions about security investments, such as selecting the right technologies and tools to protect against specific threats.

Furthermore, the sharing of CTI within the cybersecurity community can strengthen collective defenses. By collaborating and sharing threat intelligence with peers, industry partners, and government agencies, organizations can contribute to a broader effort to identify and combat cyber threats. This collaborative approach enables a faster response to emerging threats and promotes the development of more robust cybersecurity measures.

In conclusion, applying cyber threat intelligence is an indispensable component of modern cybersecurity defense strategies. It empowers organizations to proactively detect and prevent threats, respond effectively to incidents, understand their adversaries, and make informed decisions about security investments. By leveraging CTI, organizations can strengthen their defenses in an ever-evolving and increasingly perilous digital landscape, ultimately reducing the risk of cyberattacks and their associated consequences. As the cyber threat landscape evolves, applying CTI will remain critical in safeguarding our digital world.

CHAPTER V

Vulnerability Assessment and Management

Identifying vulnerabilities

Cybersecurity has become an integral part of our digital age, as organizations and individuals rely on technology for various aspects of their lives. Cyberthreats are evolving along with technology. Identifying vulnerabilities in cybersecurity is a fundamental step in protecting systems and data from potential breaches and attacks. These vulnerabilities can be found in various areas, from technical weaknesses to human errors.

Technical vulnerabilities are the most common and widely recognized in cybersecurity. These weaknesses often stem from outdated software, unpatched systems, and misconfigurations. Obsolete software and unpatched systems can expose vulnerabilities that malicious actors can exploit to obtain unauthorized access or launch attacks. Identifying and addressing these issues requires regular system maintenance, software updates, and a robust patch management process. Additionally, proper configuration management ensures that systems are set up securely and in line with best practices, reducing the risk of vulnerabilities.

Beyond technical aspects, human errors and behaviors can introduce vulnerabilities into the cybersecurity landscape. Employees, often the weakest link, can inadvertently cause security breaches by falling victim to phishing attacks, sharing sensitive information with unauthorized parties, or using weak passwords. Finding these vulnerabilities entails adopting security policies and access restrictions to reduce the risk of human error as well as educating and training staff on cybersecurity best practices.

Another critical area of vulnerability lies in the supply chain. Organizations often rely on third-party vendors and suppliers for various products and services, and these relationships can introduce cybersecurity risks. Third-party vulnerabilities can be exploited to compromise an organization's security. To identify and mitigate these risks, organizations should conduct thorough assessments of their supply chain partners, assess their cybersecurity practices, and establish precise security requirements and expectations.

Furthermore, the Internet of Things (IoT) presents a growing area of concern in identifying vulnerabilities. IoT devices are often integrated into networks without adequate security measures. These devices can be vulnerable to attacks due to weak authentication mechanisms, unencrypted communication, and a lack of security updates. Identifying vulnerabilities in IoT requires robust device management, ensuring that IoT devices are regularly updated, properly configured, and monitored for suspicious activities.

Software vulnerabilities represent another significant area of concern. As software becomes more complex, identifying and patching vulnerabilities becomes more challenging. Zero-day vulnerabilities, in particular, pose a considerable risk, as they are unknown to the software vendor and can be exploited before patches are available. Organizations should employ vulnerability scanning and penetration testing to address software vulnerabilities and monitor threat intelligence sources for information about newly discovered vulnerabilities.

Moreover, the increasing complexity of modern IT environments, including cloud computing and hybrid infrastructures, introduces additional challenges in identifying vulnerabilities. Cloud environments can present unique security risks, such as misconfigured cloud services or unauthorized access to cloud data. Identifying vulnerabilities in cloud environments requires specialized tools and expertise to assess configurations and access controls.

In conclusion, identifying vulnerabilities in cybersecurity is a critical aspect of safeguarding digital assets and data. These vulnerabilities can exist in technical aspects, human behaviors, supply chains, IoT devices, software, and complex IT environments. A comprehensive approach to identifying vulnerabilities involves a combination of technical assessments, security education and training, supply chain scrutiny, IoT device management, software patching, and vigilant monitoring. In a constantly evolving threat landscape, organizations must remain proactive and attentive in identifying and mitigating vulnerabilities to protect against cyberattacks and data breaches. Effective vulnerability management is a cornerstone of a robust cybersecurity posture in our interconnected world.

Vulnerability scanning and assessment tools

In the ever-evolving landscape of cybersecurity, identifying and mitigating vulnerabilities are paramount to safeguarding digital assets and data. Vulnerability scanning and assessment tools are crucial in this process, helping organizations proactively identify weaknesses in their systems, applications, and networks. These tools provide valuable insights into potential security risks, enabling organizations to take preemptive measures to mitigate vulnerabilities and strengthen their overall cybersecurity posture.

Vulnerability scanning tools are designed to systematically scan an organization's IT infrastructure, including servers, workstations, network devices, and applications, in search of known vulnerabilities. These tools rely on extensive databases of known vulnerabilities and their associated patches or remediation steps. By comparing the configuration and software versions of scanned assets against this database, vulnerability scanners can identify present vulnerabilities that need attention.

One of the critical advantages of vulnerability scanning tools is their ability to automate the assessment process. They can scan large and complex networks swiftly, providing organizations with a comprehensive view of their vulnerabilities. This automation saves time and ensures consistency in the assessment process, reducing the likelihood of human error.

Another valuable aspect of vulnerability scanning tools is their ability to prioritize identified vulnerabilities based on their severity and potential impact. Vulnerabilities are typically categorized using metrics like the Common Vulnerability Scoring System (or CVSS), which assigns a numerical score to each vulnerability. This scoring system helps organizations focus their remediation efforts on the most crucial vulnerabilities that pose the highest risk. Beyond identifying known vulnerabilities, some advanced vulnerability assessment tools offer additional features, such as configuration auditing and compliance checks. These tools can assess whether systems and devices are configured securely and comply with industry standards and regulatory requirements. This functionality is essential for organizations operating in highly regulated industries like finance and healthcare.

While vulnerability scanning tools are highly effective at identifying known vulnerabilities, they have limitations. They cannot detect zero-day vulnerabilities, which are unknown and unpatched vulnerabilities that attackers may exploit. Organizations often complement vulnerability scanning with other security measures, such as intrusion detection systems and threat intelligence feeds, to address this limitation.

In addition to vulnerability scanning, organizations may employ penetration testing as a more advanced form of vulnerability assessment. Penetration testing involves simulating real-world cyberattacks to assess the resilience of an organization's defenses. Unlike vulnerability scanning, penetration testing is performed by skilled cybersecurity professionals who attempt to exploit vulnerabilities in a controlled and ethical manner.

It's worth noting that vulnerability scanning and assessment tools come in various forms, from open-source to commercial solutions. Some popular commercial vulnerability scanning tools include Qualys, Tenable Nessus, and Rapid7 Nexpose, while open-source options like OpenVAS offer cost-effective alternatives. The choice of tool depends on an organization's specific needs, budget, and technical expertise.

In conclusion, vulnerability scanning and assessment tools are essential to a comprehensive cybersecurity strategy. They enable organizations to systematically identify and prioritize vulnerabilities, empowering them to take proactive measures to reduce their exposure to cyber threats. While these tools are invaluable for identifying known vulnerabilities, organizations should also remain vigilant and employ other security measures to address zero-day vulnerabilities and emerging threats. In an ever-changing cybersecurity landscape, using vulnerability scanning and assessment tools effectively is critical to maintaining the security and integrity of digital assets and data.

Strategies for managing vulnerabilities

In the realm of cybersecurity, the management of vulnerabilities is a critical aspect of safeguarding an organization's digital assets and data. Vulnerabilities, which can take many forms in an organization's IT infrastructure, allow hackers to exploit security holes and obtain access without authorization. Organizations need to implement comprehensive strategies to effectively manage vulnerabilities that encompass detection, assessment, prioritization, remediation, and continuous monitoring.

One of the primary strategies for managing vulnerabilities is regular vulnerability scanning and assessment. Organizations employ automated scanning tools to systematically inspect their network, systems, and applications for known vulnerabilities. These tools rely on extensive databases of known vulnerabilities, comparing the configuration and software versions of scanned assets against this database to identify weaknesses. Vulnerability scanning provides a baseline assessment of an organization's security posture and helps identify areas that require attention.

Once vulnerabilities are identified, prioritization becomes crucial. Not all vulnerabilities are equal; some pose a higher risk than others. Vulnerability management tools often assign severity scores based on metrics like the Common Vulnerability Scoring System (CVSS), allowing organizations to prioritize remediation efforts on the most critical vulnerabilities that pose the most significant risk to their operations. This prioritization ensures that resources are allocated efficiently to address the most pressing security concerns.

Remediation is fixing or mitigating vulnerabilities to reduce the associated risk. This step involves deploying patches, updating software, reconfiguring systems, or implementing additional security controls. Effective remediation requires coordination between IT and security teams to ensure that vulnerabilities are addressed promptly and without disrupting essential business operations.

In addition to vulnerability scanning and remediation, organizations can benefit from proactive measures like penetration testing and red team exercises. Penetration testing involves simulated attacks by ethical hackers to uncover vulnerabilities and assess an organization's ability to defend against real-world threats. Red team exercises take this a step further by conducting comprehensive assessments that simulate advanced persistent threats. These activities help organizations identify vulnerabilities that automated scanning tools may miss and provide insights into their security resilience.

Continuous monitoring is another vital aspect of vulnerability management. Cyber threats evolve rapidly, and new vulnerabilities are discovered regularly. Therefore, organizations must maintain vigilance by continuously monitoring their systems for emerging vulnerabilities and potential indicators of compromise. Tools like intrusion detection systems, threat intelligence feeds, and security information and event management systems are frequently employed for this purpose.

One essential element of vulnerability remediation is patch management. Organizations must establish robust processes for applying patches promptly and efficiently. This includes testing patches in a controlled environment to ensure they do not introduce new issues before deployment. Automation tools can streamline the patch management process, making it easier to keep systems up-to-date.

Furthermore, organizations should consider the human factor in vulnerability management. Employee training and awareness programs are vital to reduce human error and the introduction of vulnerabilities through negligent or malicious actions. Educating staff about common attack vectors, phishing awareness, and the importance of strong passwords can significantly enhance an organization's security posture.

Finally, vulnerability management should be integral to an organization's overall cybersecurity strategy. It should align with security policies and compliance requirements, with clear roles and responsibilities for various teams and stakeholders. Regular reporting and communication about vulnerability management progress and findings should be established to ensure transparency and accountability.

In conclusion, managing vulnerabilities is a multifaceted endeavor that demands a comprehensive strategy encompassing detection, assessment, prioritization, remediation, and continuous monitoring. Organizations must stay proactive in their approach, using a combination of automated scanning tools, penetration testing, and employee training to mitigate vulnerabilities effectively. Additionally, strong coordination between IT and security teams and compliance with industry standards and regulations is crucial in building a robust vulnerability management program. In today's dynamic threat landscape, effective vulnerability management is essential to maintaining the security and resilience of an organization's digital infrastructure.

CHAPTER VI

Penetration Testing

What is penetration testing?

In the ever-evolving landscape of cybersecurity, organizations face increasing threats and vulnerabilities. To proactively identify and address potential weaknesses in their systems and defenses, many organizations turn to penetration testing, also known as ethical hacking. Penetration testing is a systematic and controlled process where cybersecurity professionals simulate real-world cyberattacks to assess the security posture of an organization's digital infrastructure.

Penetration testing aims to detect vulnerabilities and weaknesses in an organization's systems, applications, networks, and devices before malicious actors can exploit them. This proactive approach allows organizations to shore up their defenses, patch vulnerabilities, and improve their overall cybersecurity posture. Penetration testers, often called ethical hackers, use their skills and knowledge to mimic the tactics, techniques, and procedures (TTPs) of malicious hackers without causing harm to the organization's assets.

The penetration testing process typically follows several key phases. The first phase involves scoping and planning, where the objectives and scope of the test are defined. This includes identifying the specific systems, applications, and networks to be tested, as well as setting rules of engagement and obtaining necessary permissions from stakeholders.

Next comes the reconnaissance phase, where penetration testers gather information about the target environment. This information can entail details about the organization's infrastructure, employees, and potential vulnerabilities. The goal is to simulate how an attacker might gather intelligence before launching an attack. Once sufficient information is gathered, the penetration testers move on to the scanning and enumeration phase. They use various tools and techniques to scan the target environment for open ports, services, and potential vulnerabilities. Enumeration involves identifying active hosts, user accounts, and system configurations vulnerable to exploitation.

In the exploitation phase, the penetration testers attempt to leverage identified vulnerabilities to gain unauthorized access or compromise systems. This phase simulates the actual attack, and ethical hackers use their expertise to exploit vulnerabilities without causing damage or data loss.

After successfully exploiting vulnerabilities, penetration testers move on to the post-exploitation phase. Here, they assess the extent of the compromise, escalate privileges, and demonstrate the potential impact of a successful attack. This phase helps organizations understand the severity of vulnerabilities and their possible consequences.

The final phase of penetration testing is reporting. Penetration testers provide detailed reports to the organization's stakeholders, outlining the vulnerabilities discovered, their potential impact, and recommendations for remediation. These reports serve as a roadmap for organizations to prioritize and address security weaknesses.

Penetration testing offers several valuable benefits to organizations. First and foremost, it helps identify vulnerabilities and weaknesses that may be challenging to detect through automated scanning tools alone. Penetration testers can uncover complex issues, misconfigurations, and potential security gaps that automated tools might overlook.

Furthermore, penetration testing provides insights into an organization's incident response capabilities. Organizations can evaluate how well they detect, respond to, and mitigate security incidents by simulating attacks. This information can be utilized to improve incident response procedures and training.

Additionally, penetration testing helps organizations meet regulatory compliance requirements. Many industry regulations and standards, like the PCI DSS and HIPAA, mandate regular security testing and assessments. Penetration testing allows organizations demonstrate compliance by identifying and addressing vulnerabilities.

In conclusion, penetration testing is vital to a comprehensive cybersecurity strategy. It enables organizations to proactively determine and address vulnerabilities, improve security posture, and enhance incident response capabilities. By simulating real-world cyberattacks, penetration testing provides valuable insights to help organizations protect their digital assets and data in an increasingly complex and dangerous threat landscape.

Types of penetration testing (Black Box, White Box, Grey Box)

Penetration testing, sometimes called ethical hacking, is a vital part of modern cybersecurity tactics because it helps companies find vulnerabilities and flaws in their digital infrastructure before bad actors can take advantage of them. There are many different types of penetration testing, and each has its own approach and degree of access to the target system. Black Box, White Box, and also Grey Box testing are the three main types of penetration testing, and each has a specific function in the endeavor to improve an organization's security posture.

Black Box testing is designed to replicate an external attacker's perspective. In this approach, the penetration tester is provided with little to no prior knowledge about the target system or its inner workings. The tester's objective is to simulate an attack without any internal information. This testing method closely mirrors the experience of a real-world attacker, making it valuable for assessing an organization's external security defenses.

During Black Box testing, the tester starts with minimal information, such as the organization's public-facing systems and web applications. They attempt to identify vulnerabilities, gain unauthorized access, and escalate privileges as an external attacker would. This type of testing can reveal how well an organization's security controls, such as firewalls and intrusion detection systems, protect against external threats.

White Box testing, or clear box or glass box testing, takes the opposite approach by providing the penetration tester with full knowledge of the target system's internal architecture, source code, and configurations. This level of insight allows the tester to perform an in-depth and detailed assessment of the system's security.

In White Box testing, the penetration tester leverages knowledge of the system's architecture and code to identify vulnerabilities from an insider's perspective. This approach is beneficial for evaluating the robustness of an organization's internal security measures, including the effectiveness of access controls and authentication mechanisms. White Box testing is often applied to applications that require a high level of security, such as financial software and healthcare systems.

Grey Box testing balances Black Box and White Box testing, offering the penetration tester a partial view of the target system. In Grey Box testing, the tester has some knowledge of the target environment, but not to the extent provided in White Box testing. This partial knowledge might include system architecture, network diagrams, or limited access credentials.

Grey Box testing is flexible and adaptable, making it suitable for various scenarios. Testers can focus on specific areas of concern while exploring the system's external facets. This approach allows organizations to assess the security of critical components while maintaining a degree of realism, similar to Black Box testing.

Each type of penetration testing has its advantages and use cases. Black Box testing mimics external threats and assesses the effectiveness of perimeter defenses. White Box testing provides an in-depth analysis of internal security controls and code vulnerabilities. Grey Box testing combines elements of both, offering flexibility and tailored assessments.

In conclusion, penetration testing is a crucial practice in modern cybersecurity, and organizations must select the most appropriate type of testing based on their goals and the specific assets they want to protect. Whether it's Black Box, White Box, or Grey Box testing, the ultimate aim is to proactively identify vulnerabilities, weaknesses, and security gaps to fortify an organization's defenses and minimize the risk of cyberattacks. By embracing these testing methodologies, organizations can bolster their cybersecurity posture and stay resilient in the face of evolving threats.

Conducting a penetration test

Conducting a penetration test is an essential practice in cybersecurity, serving as a proactive measure to identify vulnerabilities and weaknesses in an organization's digital infrastructure before malicious actors can exploit them. This systematic and structured approach to ethical hacking involves several key phases, each contributing to a comprehensive assessment of an organization's security posture.

The planning and scoping phase is the first and crucial step in conducting a penetration test. During this phase, the objectives and scope of the assessment are defined in close collaboration between the organization and the penetration testing team. Clear objectives outline what the organization aims to achieve from the test, while the scope specifies the systems, applications, and networks to be included in the assessment. During this phase, legal and compliance considerations are addressed, and necessary permissions are obtained to avoid any legal complications.

Following the planning phase, reconnaissance takes place. This phase entails gathering information about the target environment, mirroring how an attacker might gather intelligence before launching an attack. Various techniques, such as open-source intelligence gathering and network scanning, are employed to gain insights into the target's attack surface.

Building on the information gathered during reconnaissance, the penetration testers move on to the scanning and enumeration phase. Specialized tools are used to scan the target environment for open ports, services, and potential vulnerabilities. Enumeration, on the other hand, involves identifying active hosts, user accounts, and system configurations that may be vulnerable to exploitation. This phase is crucial for pinpointing potential entry points for attacks.

As the assessment progresses, the exploitation phase is where penetration testers attempt to leverage the identified vulnerabilities to gain unauthorized access or compromise systems. This phase effectively simulates an actual attack, with ethical hackers utilizing their expertise to exploit vulnerabilities without causing any harm or data loss. The primary goal here is to demonstrate how an attacker could compromise the organization's assets. Post-exploitation follows the successful exploitation of vulnerabilities. In this phase, penetration testers assess the extent of the compromise, escalate privileges, and demonstrate the potential impact of a successful attack. This information is invaluable in helping organizations understand the severity of vulnerabilities and the possible consequences of a security breach. It also includes validating whether sensitive data can be accessed or exfiltrated.

The final phase in conducting a penetration test is reporting. Penetration testers provide detailed reports to the organization's stakeholders, outlining the vulnerabilities discovered, their potential impact, and recommendations for remediation. These reports serve as a roadmap for organizations to effectively prioritize and address security weaknesses. Clear and actionable reports are crucial to ensure that vulnerabilities are adequately addressed and that the organization can enhance its security posture.

Conducting a penetration test is a collaborative effort that necessitates close coordination between the organization and the testing team. Choosing experienced and certified penetration testers who adhere to ethical guidelines and industry best practices is essential. Moreover, organizations should view penetration testing as an iterative process, conducting assessments regularly to stay ahead of evolving cyber threats and vulnerabilities.

In conclusion, penetration testing is an indispensable component of a comprehensive cybersecurity strategy. It gives organizations valuable insights into their security posture, enabling them to identify and mitigate potential risks proactively. Organizations can bolster their defenses and minimize the risk of cyberattacks by following a structured approach that encompasses planning, reconnaissance, scanning, exploitation, post-exploitation, and reporting. Regular penetration tests are essential in an ever-changing threat landscape, ensuring an organization's digital assets remain secure and resilient.

CHAPTER VII

Network Security

Network security fundamentals

The foundation of cybersecurity in the modern digital era is network security. It is a comprehensive approach encompassing various strategies, technologies, and practices to safeguard an organization's digital assets, data, and network infrastructure from myriad threats. Fundamentally, network security revolves around three core principles: confidentiality, integrity, and availability.

The cornerstone of network security is confidentiality, which makes sure that private data is protected from prying eyes. Encryption, a fundamental technique in achieving confidentiality, transforms data into an unreadable format, ensuring only authorized parties possess the necessary decryption keys. Secure communication protocols like HTTPS, SSH, and VPNs heavily rely on encryption to protect data as it traverses networks.

Integrity ensures that data remains unaltered during storage or transmission. Hash functions and digital signatures serve as critical tools for maintaining data integrity. Hash functions create unique fingerprints, or hashes, for data, enabling recipients to validate its integrity and ensure it hasn't been tampered with. Digital signatures, on the other hand, verify data authenticity and sender identity, bolstering confidence in data integrity.

Availability guarantees that network resources and services are accessible when needed. Attacks such as Denial-of-Service (DoS) and Distributed Denial-of- Service (DDoS) strive to disrupt availability by overwhelming networks or services, rendering them inaccessible to legitimate users. Network security measures, including intrusion detection systems as well as firewalls, play pivotal roles in detecting and mitigating such attacks safeguarding resource availability.

Authentication is verifying the identity of users or systems seeking network access. Robust authentication methods like the two-factor authentication (2FA) and biometrics enhance security by requiring multiple verification forms, reducing the risk of unauthorized access. While widely used, passwords can be vulnerable if not adequately managed, underlining the importance of robust authentication mechanisms.

Authorization determines what actions or resources authenticated users or systems can access within the network. Access control lists (or ACLs) and role-based access control (or RBAC) are standard tools for enforcing authorization policies, ensuring users only have access to resources pertinent to their roles.

Network segmentation, an emerging best practice, involves dividing networks into isolated segments or zones. This containment strategy limits lateral movement for attackers, as even if one part of the network is compromised, access to other segments remains restricted. Sensitive data, for instance, can be stored in a highly restricted segment, enhancing its protection.

System components that are essential to network security include intrusion detection and prevention systems (or IDS/IPS). By monitoring network traffic for odd or suspicious activities, IDS creates alerts that security professionals can look into. IPS goes one step further by improving security posture and proactively preventing or mitigating threats that are detected.

By using patch management, network security is kept resistant to known vulnerabilities. Frequent software and system upgrades and patches are necessary to fix known vulnerabilities and lower the attack surface. If this is neglected, networks may be vulnerable to cyberattacks by malicious actors.

Finally, security awareness is an integral factor in network security. Human error remains a significant security vulnerability, making security training and education programs critical. Phishing awareness, password hygiene, and recognizing social engineering attempts are vital aspects of user-focused network security.

In conclusion, network security fundamentals embody a multi-pronged approach to protect data and resources' confidentiality, integrity, and availability within a network. These principles underpin encryption, authentication, authorization, network segmentation, intrusion detection and prevention, and security awareness. Maintaining robust network security requires ongoing diligence, education, and adaptability as the cybersecurity landscape evolves. Organizations and individuals must remain vigilant and informed about emerging threats and best practices to defend against cyber risks in our interconnected world effectively.

Securing Wi-Fi networks

Wi-Fi networks have become indispensable in our increasingly connected world, serving as the backbone of our digital interactions. Wi-Fi provides convenient and wireless access to the internet and local resources, whether in homes, businesses, or public spaces. However, the convenience of Wi-Fi comes with significant security challenges. Securing Wi-Fi networks is paramount to safeguard sensitive data, protect network integrity, and ensure user privacy.

One of the fundamental steps in securing a Wi-Fi network is setting a strong and unique password for the router. The password should be complex, combining upper and lower-case letters, numbers, and special characters. It's crucial to avoid using default or easily guessable passwords. Enabling encryption protocols like WPA3 (Wi-Fi Protected Access 3) or WPA2 ensures that data transmitted between devices and the router is encrypted. This encryption significantly raises the bar for cybercriminals attempting to intercept and decipher the data.

Changing default router credentials is another vital step in securing a Wi-Fi network. Manufacturers often set default usernames and passwords for routers, which are widely known and documented. Failing to change these default credentials can leave the router vulnerable to unauthorized access, potentially leading to severe security breaches.

Beyond password protection, it's essential to enable advanced security protocols such as WPA3 and WPA2. These protocols encrypt data and employ advanced security techniques to authenticate devices and safeguard against various types of attacks, including brute force and dictionary attacks.

To further enhance security, hiding the Service Set Identifier (SSID), also known as "SSID cloaking," can be considered. While this measure won't deter determined attackers, it can make it less convenient for casual Wi-Fi leeches to discover and connect to the network.

MAC (Media Access Control) address filtering is an additional layer of security. It allows network administrators to specify which devices can connect to the network based on their unique MAC addresses. While this method is not foolproof (as MAC addresses can be spoofed), it does add an extra obstacle for unauthorized access.

Regularly updating a router's firmware is essential for addressing known vulnerabilities and improving its performance. Manufacturers release firmware updates to patch security vulnerabilities, and keeping the router's firmware up-to-date is crucial to ensure that these known weaknesses are promptly addressed.

Creating separate guest networks is another valuable security practice. Many modern routers offer this feature, which isolates guest devices from the primary network, preventing them from accessing sensitive data and resources. It's an excellent way to provide internet access to visitors while enhancing network security.

Strong firewalls and intrusion detection capabilities are often built into routers. These should be appropriately configured and updated to protect against common network threats. In some cases, third-party firewall solutions can offer advanced security features.

Lastly, it's advisable to turn off remote management of the router unless necessary. Allowing remote access can open up security vulnerabilities, as attackers could exploit this feature to gain unauthorized control over the network.

In conclusion, securing Wi-Fi networks is imperative to mitigate the growing range of cyber threats and vulnerabilities. Individuals and organizations can significantly bolster their Wi-Fi security by implementing strong passwords, enabling network encryption, changing default router credentials, and using advanced security protocols. Additional practices, such as hiding the SSID, MAC address filtering, firmware updates, and using guest networks, all contribute to a stronger security posture. Regular monitoring, firewalls, and intrusion detection mechanisms are essential for ongoing network security maintenance. By following these best practices, Wi-Fi users can enjoy the benefits of wireless connectivity while safeguarding their digital assets and privacy.

Firewalls, IDS, and IPS systems

In the ever-evolving landscape of cybersecurity, organizations face constant threats and vulnerabilities that put their digital assets and data at risk. They rely on security measures to mitigate these risks, including firewalls, Intrusion Detection Systems (IDS), and Intrusion Prevention Systems (IPS). These critical components form a robust defense strategy that helps organizations safeguard their networks, systems, and sensitive information.

In terms of network security, firewalls are the first line of protection. They provide as a line of defense between a reliable internal network and an unreliable external network, such as the internet. In order to decide whether to allow, block, or route incoming and outgoing network traffic, firewalls look at the data and apply established rules. These regulations may be based on application protocols, port numbers, or IP addresses.

Hardware and software firewalls are the two main types of firewalls. Hardware firewalls are typically deployed at the network perimeter, safeguarding an entire network. In contrast, software firewalls are installed on individual devices, such as computers or smartphones, providing a layer of protection specific to each device.

Firewalls prevent unauthorized access, block malicious traffic, and reduce the attack surface. They effectively thwart common threats like port scans, unauthorized access attempts, and known malware communication. While firewalls act as gatekeepers, Intrusion Detection Systems (IDS) function as vigilant sentinels within a network. IDS monitors network traffic for suspicious or anomalous activity that may indicate a security breach. These systems employ various methods to identify potential threats, such as signature-based and anomaly-based detection.

Signature-based IDS relies on a database of predefined attack signatures or patterns. When network traffic matches these signatures, an alert is triggered. This method effectively detects known threats but may miss novel or zero-day attacks.

Anomaly-based IDS, on the other hand, establishes a baseline of normal network behavior. Any deviation from this baseline is flagged as potentially suspicious. While this approach is more adaptable to new threats, it may also generate false positives.

IDS systems provide organizations with real-time insights into their network's security status. When a potential intrusion or security incident is detected, the IDS generates alerts that security personnel can investigate further. IDS helps organizations respond promptly and mitigate potential damage by identifying threats in their early stages.

Intrusion Prevention Systems (IPS) are the next evolution in network security after IDS. While IDS focuses on detection and alerting, IPS takes a more proactive approach by actively blocking and mitigating threats in real time.

IPS systems use the same detection methods as IDS but go a step further by taking automated actions to prevent the detected threats from succeeding. For example, suppose an IPS detects a suspicious network packet. In that case, it can immediately block that packet from entering the network or disrupt the communication between an attacker and a compromised system.

IPS systems effectively stop threats before they can cause harm, reduce the burden on security teams, and minimize the impact of cyberattacks. However, they require careful configuration and tuning to avoid false positives, which can disrupt legitimate network traffic.

In conclusion, firewalls, IDS, and IPS systems are essential to modern cybersecurity strategies. Firewalls act as gatekeepers, controlling traffic in and out of networks, while IDS and IPS systems monitor for suspicious activity and take proactive measures to detect and prevent intrusions. These technologies work in tandem to provide a multi-layered defense that helps organizations protect their networks, systems, and data from various threats. As the threat landscape continues to evolve, firewalls, IDS, and IPS systems remain critical in maintaining the security and integrity of digital assets and information.

CHAPTER VIII

Web Application Security

Common web application vulnerabilities

Our digital lives would not be the same without web applications, which allow us to do anything from social networking and shopping to banking and productivity. However, their ubiquity and complexity make them a prime target for cyberattacks. It is essential to understand and address common web application vulnerabilities to ensure the security and integrity of these applications.

Injection attacks are among the most prevalent web application vulnerabilities. These attacks occur when untrusted data is inserted into a command or query that an interpreter executes. SQL Injection (SQLi) and Cross-Site Scripting (XSS) are two prominent examples. SQLi allows attackers to manipulate a web application's database, potentially gaining unauthorized access to sensitive data or executing malicious commands. Conversely, XSS entails inserting dangerous scripts into other users' web pages, jeopardizing their data or browser sessions.

Cross-Site Request Forgery (CSRF) attacks are another common threat. They deceive users into executing malicious actions in web applications without their knowledge or consent. Attackers exploit a website's trust in a user's browser by crafting a malicious request that the user unwittingly submits, leading to unintended actions such as changing account settings or making unauthorized transactions.

Weak authentication and session management practices can expose web applications to significant vulnerabilities. Inadequate protection of credentials, poor session management, and predictable session tokens can result in unauthorized access, account hijacking, or session fixation attacks.

Security misconfigurations are a persistent issue. They arise from incomplete or lax web servers, databases, or application frameworks configurations. Attackers can exploit these misconfigurations to gain unauthorized access, execute arbitrary code, or compromise the application's security. Regular configuration audits and adherence to best practices are essential to mitigate these vulnerabilities.

Insecure deserialization vulnerabilities occur when an application parses data from an unreliable source without proper validation. Attackers can manipulate serialized objects to execute arbitrary code, potentially leading to remote code execution, privilege escalation, or data manipulation.

Broken access control occurs when an application fails to enforce proper restrictions on authenticated users. It may result in unlawful access to private information or sensitive locations, giving users the ability to carry out tasks for which they are not permitted. Robust access control mechanisms, such as Role-Based Access Control (RBAC), are essential to prevent such vulnerabilities.

XML External Entity (XXE) attacks target applications processing XML input, allowing attackers to exploit vulnerabilities in XML parsing. By injecting malicious XML entities, attackers can disclose internal files, perform denial-of-service attacks, or execute arbitrary code.

Lack of proper security headers can leave web applications vulnerable to attacks such as Cross-Site Scripting (XSS) and Clickjacking. Implementing headers like Content Security Policy (CSP), Strict Transport Security (HSTS), and X-Frame-Options can help mitigate these risks.

Unvalidated redirects and forwards in web applications can lead to phishing attacks. Attackers craft malicious links that redirect users to fraudulent websites, compromising their credentials or injecting malicious code.

Addressing these common web application vulnerabilities requires a multifaceted approach. Developers must adopt secure coding practices, implement input validation, and sanitize user inputs to prevent injection attacks. Robust authentication and session management mechanisms should be in place to mitigate broken authentication and session management vulnerabilities. Security configurations must be routinely audited, and secure deserialization practices must be adopted to prevent security misconfigurations and insecure deserialization.

Moreover, implementing access control measures, securing against XXE attacks, using proper security headers, and validating redirects and forwards are vital for bolstering web application security. Regular security assessments, including penetration testing and code reviews, can help identify and remediate vulnerabilities effectively.

In conclusion, web application vulnerabilities pose significant risks to organizations and users.

Understanding and addressing these vulnerabilities is a continuous process that requires vigilance and a commitment to secure coding practices and robust security measures. By proactively identifying and mitigating common web application vulnerabilities, developers and organizations can protect their applications and data from various cyber threats, ensuring a safer online experience for all users.

Best practices for securing web applications

Web applications have become integral to our digital landscape, serving various functions from online banking and e-commerce to social networking and productivity tools. However, the prevalence of web applications also makes them lucrative targets for cyberattacks. To safeguard sensitive data, protect user privacy, and maintain the trust of customers, it is crucial to adhere to best practices for securing web applications.

Input validation and sanitization are foundational principles in web application security. Developers must rigorously validate and sanitize user inputs to prevent malicious code injection, such as SQL injection (SQLi) and Cross-Site Scripting (XSS). Web applications can effectively mitigate these common attack vectors by filtering, escaping, or encoding user inputs.

Authentication and authorization are pivotal for controlling access to web applications. Robust authentication mechanisms, including strong password policies and multi-factor authentication (MFA), ensure that only authorized users can access sensitive information. Authorization mechanisms, such as Role-Based Access Control (or RBAC), restrict users' privileges based on their roles, preventing unauthorized actions.

Secure communication is paramount to protect data in transit. Implementing Secure Socket Layer (SSL) or Transport Layer Security (TLS) is necessary to encrypt data during transmission, guarding against eavesdropping and man-in-the-middle attacks. Enforcing HTTPS for all communications, including login pages and data exchanges, is a best practice for ensuring secure connections.

Security headers play a crucial role in enhancing web application security. Content Security Policy (CSP), Strict Transport Security (HSTS), and X-Content-Type-Options are security headers that help prevent attacks like XSS and content sniffing. Properly configured security headers reduce the attack surface, bolstering security.

Security patch management is essential to address known vulnerabilities. Regularly updating software, frameworks, libraries, and third-party components helps mitigate the risk of exploitation. Attackers often target outdated or unpatched software, making timely updates crucial.

Comprehensive security logging and monitoring are vital for detecting and responding to security incidents. Security logs can uncover suspicious activities, while automated monitoring tools can identify anomalies and trigger alerts. Effective incident response relies on timely detection, investigation, and mitigation.

Session management is critical to web application security. Secure generation and handling of session tokens, protection against session fixation attacks, and proper cookie management ensure that sessions remain safe and free from tampering or data leakage.

Web Application Firewalls (WAFs) provide an additional layer of protection. They filter malicious traffic and defend against common web application attacks. WAFs can be configured to block or log potentially harmful requests, adding an extra safeguard against threats.

Error handling is another aspect that should be considered. Error messages should provide minimal information to users to avoid disclosing sensitive data. Simultaneously, comprehensive error logs should capture detailed information for system administrators and security teams to diagnose and address issues swiftly.

Regular security testing is imperative to identify vulnerabilities proactively. Penetration testing, code reviews, and automated vulnerability scanning help uncover weaknesses in the application. Implementing a secure development lifecycle (SDL) ensures that security is integral to the development process.

Lastly, security training and awareness programs are crucial to educate development teams and stakeholders about potential threats and safe coding practices. Ensuring that everyone involved understands security best practices and knows how to respond effectively to security incidents is fundamental in maintaining web application security.

In conclusion, securing web applications is a multifaceted endeavor that demands a comprehensive approach. Organizations can mitigate common security risks by adhering to best practices, such as input validation, robust authentication, secure communication, and proactive security testing. Implementing security headers, session management, and Web Application Firewalls enhances the overall security posture. Security logging, patch management, and error handling are essential for effective security. Lastly, ongoing security training and awareness programs foster a security-conscious culture that helps protect web applications, safeguard sensitive data, and maintain user trust in an ever-evolving threat landscape.

Web application security tools and testing

In today's digital landscape, web applications have become essential to our daily lives, providing a wide range of online services and functionalities. However, the increasing complexity of web applications and the ever- evolving threat landscape have made them attractive targets for cyberattacks. Organizations rely on a combination of web application security tools and testing methodologies to ensure the security and integrity of web applications.

Web application security tools encompass a broad spectrum of software solutions designed to identify and mitigate security vulnerabilities within web applications. These tools automate the process of scanning, testing, and monitoring for potential threats. These tools include web vulnerability scanners, such as Burp Suite and Acunetix, automatically identifying common security issues like SQL injection, Cross-Site Scripting (XSS), and security misconfigurations. Additionally, web application firewalls (WAFs) act as a protective barrier, inspecting incoming traffic and blocking malicious requests to prevent attacks.

Static Application Security Testing (SAST) tools, such as Checkmarx and Veracode, analyze the source code or binary code of web applications to identify security vulnerabilities at an early stage of development. These tools focus on code-level issues like insecure coding practices and potential vulnerabilities. Dynamic Application Security Testing (DAST) tools, like Netsparker and Qualys Web Application Scanning, assess running web applications by sending requests and analyzing responses, identifying vulnerabilities in the application's runtime environment.

Interactive Application Security Testing (IAST) tools, including Contrast Security and Checkmarx SCA, combine elements of both SAST and DAST. They interact with the running application to identify vulnerabilities while analyzing the source code. This approach provides a comprehensive assessment of application security.

In addition to web application security tools, organizations employ various testing methodologies to assess the security of their web applications. Penetration testing, often called ethical hacking, involves authorized attempts to exploit vulnerabilities in a web application to evaluate its security posture. Skilled penetration testers simulate real-world attack scenarios to identify weaknesses malicious actors might exploit.

On the other hand, code reviews involve manual inspection of the application's source code by security experts or developers. This approach helps uncover code-level vulnerabilities, insecure coding practices, and areas where security improvements can be made.

Threat modeling is a proactive approach to determining potential security threats and vulnerabilities during a web application's design and development phases. It aids in making informed security decisions and prioritizing security measures.

Security scanning tools, both automated and manual, systematically scan web applications for known vulnerabilities and configuration issues. These tools provide a quick assessment of security weaknesses.

Security headers and configuration settings are crucial for web application security. Testing tools like securityheaders.com and Mozilla Observatory assess the presence and adequacy of security headers and provide recommendations for improvements.

As web applications increasingly rely on APIs (Application Programming Interfaces), testing the security of these interfaces is essential. Specialized API security testing tools and techniques assess authentication, authorization, and data protection in APIs.

In conclusion, web application security is a multifaceted challenge that requires a comprehensive approach. Organizations must employ a combination of web application security tools and testing methodologies to identify and remediate vulnerabilities effectively. These tools and methodologies help organizations proactively enhance the security of their web applications, protect sensitive data, and maintain user trust in an increasingly digital world.

CHAPTER IX

Cloud Security

The importance of cloud security

In today's digital era, adopting cloud computing has transformed businesses' operations, offering them unprecedented scalability, flexibility, and cost-efficiency. However, this shift towards the cloud has also brought forth a crucial concern: the security of data, applications, and services stored in cloud environments. Since more and more businesses are depending on cloud services to store, manage, and process their vital data, the need of cloud security cannot be overstated.

One of the most compelling reasons for prioritizing cloud security is the vast amount of sensitive and confidential data that organizations entrust to cloud service providers. This data encompasses financial records, customer information, intellectual property, proprietary business data, and more. Any unauthorized access, data breach, or security lapse can have far-reaching consequences, ranging from financial losses and legal repercussions to severe damage to a company's reputation.

Cloud security encompasses many measures, practices, and technologies designed to safeguard data, applications, and the underlying cloud infrastructure. By using these security measures, data is protected from potential dangers, kept private, and available only to authorized personnel.

An essential component of cloud security measures is data protection.

Encryption and access controls are fundamental components that ensure data remains secure. Encryption techniques safeguard data in transit and at rest, rendering it unreadable to unauthorized individuals even if they manage to gain access.

Moreover, cloud security is pivotal in helping organizations meet compliance and regulatory requirements. Various industries are subject to stringent data protection regulations, such as GDPR, HIPAA, and PCI DSS. Cloud security measures provide the necessary controls, auditing capabilities, and documentation needed to demonstrate compliance with these regulations.

Furthermore, cloud security supports business continuity and disaster recovery efforts. Cloud services offer robust disaster recovery capabilities, including data replication and backup solutions. This ensures that data remains accessible, even during hardware failures, natural disasters, or other unexpected disruptions.

Scalability and flexibility are inherent benefits of cloud environments. Cloud security measures can scale and adapt to the dynamic nature of these environments. As organizations expand or contract their cloud resources, security provisions remain effective, preventing security gaps.

Threat detection and response are critical aspects of cloud security. Cloud environments are not immune to cyber threats despite their inherent security features. Advanced threat detection, monitoring, and real-time alerts are essential components that help organizations identify and respond to security incidents promptly.

Identity and access management (IAM) is another vital element of cloud security. Effective management of user identities and access privileges ensures that only the authorized personnel can access specific resources, minimizing the risk of unauthorized access.

Additionally, cloud security emphasizes the shared responsibility model. Cloud providers are in charge of securing the cloud infrastructure, such as data centers and hardware. However, customers must secure their data and applications within the cloud, highlighting the importance of implementing robust security practices and controls.

Organizations must invest in employee awareness and training programs to ensure comprehensive cloud security. Employees are significant in maintaining security, and awareness programs help educate them about best practices and potential risks associated with cloud usage.

Third-party risk management is also a key consideration. Many organizations rely on third-party cloud service providers. Managing the security of these providers is crucial, involving due diligence, security assessments, and the establishment of contractual security obligations.

In conclusion, the importance of cloud security must be addressed in today's digital landscape. While the advantages of cloud technology are numerous, they must be balanced with robust security measures to protect sensitive data and resources. Organizations must proactively implement cloud security practices encompassing data protection, compliance adherence, disaster recovery, threat detection, access management, and employee awareness. Cloud security is not merely an option; it is imperative for any organization leveraging cloud services in their digital journey. Failure to prioritize cloud security can lead to severe consequences that impact an organization's integrity, trustworthiness, and success in an increasingly interconnected and data-driven world.

Securing cloud infrastructure

The adoption of cloud computing has become ubiquitous across industries, revolutionizing how organizations store, manage, and process their data and applications. Cloud infrastructure offers numerous benefits, such as scalability, cost-efficiency, and flexibility. However, these advantages come hand in hand with the critical responsibility of securing cloud resources. Securing cloud infrastructure is a multifaceted endeavor that requires careful planning, robust practices, and a thorough understanding of the shared responsibility model between cloud service providers and customers.

One of the fundamental aspects of securing cloud infrastructure is understanding the shared responsibility model. This model delineates the responsibilities between the cloud service provider (or CSP) and the customer in a cloud environment. The CSP is in charge of securing the underlying cloud infrastructure, including data centers, physical servers, and the hypervisor layer. On the other hand, the customer is responsible for securing their data, applications, and configurations within the cloud.

Data protection is paramount in cloud security. Encryption, both in transit and at rest, plays a central role in safeguarding sensitive data. Data encryption ensures that the data remains unreadable and unusable even if unauthorized access occurs. Cloud providers typically offer encryption services, but it's the customer's responsibility to implement encryption keys and manage access controls appropriately.

Identity and access management (IAM) is another vital cloud security component. Effective IAM ensures that only authorized users and applications can access cloud resources. Role-based access control (RBAC) is a common IAM practice that assigns permissions based on users' roles, reducing the risk of unauthorized access. Multi-factor authentication (MFA) adds a further layer of security, requiring users to provide multiple verification forms.

Cloud providers offer various security features and tools that customers can leverage to enhance their security posture. Security groups as well as network access control lists (or NACLs) allow organizations to define firewall rules and control traffic flow. Intrusion detection and prevention systems help identify and mitigate suspicious activities. Cloud-native security services like AWS GuardDuty and Azure Security Center provide automated threat detection and response capabilities.

Regular security assessments and audits are indispensable for maintaining cloud security. Vulnerability assessments and penetration testing help determine weaknesses in cloud configurations and applications. These assessments should be conducted periodically, especially after significant changes or updates to cloud resources. Compliance audits ensure that security controls align with industry standards and regulatory requirements.

Security monitoring and incident response are crucial for proactive threat detection and mitigation. Cloud environments generate vast amounts of logs and telemetry data, which should be continuously monitored.

Security information and event management solutions aggregate and analyze this data, allowing organizations to identify anomalies and potential threats in real time. A well-defined incident response plan is equally crucial for swift and effective actions in a security incident.

Cloud security also entails proper management of cloud configuration. Misconfigurations are a leading reason of cloud security incidents. Continuous monitoring and automation tools can help identify and remediate misconfigurations promptly. Implementing Infrastructure as Code (IaC) practices allows organizations to define and provision cloud resources with predefined security configurations, reducing the risk of human error.

Lastly, employee training and awareness play a significant role in cloud security. Human error remains a prevalent cause of security incidents. Ensuring that employees are well-informed about cloud security best practices, potential risks, and how to report security incidents is essential.

In conclusion, securing cloud infrastructure is critical in today's digital landscape. While cloud computing offers unmatched scalability and efficiency, it also presents a shared responsibility for security between the customer and the cloud service provider. Understanding this model and implementing robust security practices, such as data encryption, IAM, security assessments, monitoring, and incident response, are essential for safeguarding cloud resources. Preventive actions, ongoing monitoring, and employee education are essential for preserving the security and integrity of cloud infrastructure. Security must continue to be the top priority as businesses depend more and more on the cloud for their digital operations in order to safeguard sensitive data and maintain business continuity.

Cloud security best practices

Organizations are adopting cloud computing at an increasing rate as they want to capitalize on its scalability, cost-effectiveness, and flexibility. However, this migration to the cloud also introduces new security challenges that organizations must address comprehensively. Adherence to cloud best practices is essential to safeguard sensitive data and maintain a secure cloud environment.

A fundamental principle in cloud security is understanding the shared responsibility model. This model delineates the responsibilities between the cloud service provider (CSP) and the customer. While CSPs are in charge of securing the underlying cloud infrastructure, customers are in charge of securing their data, applications, and configurations within the cloud. Recognizing this shared responsibility underscores the importance of implementing robust security practices at the customer's end.

Data protection is a cornerstone of cloud security. Encrypting data, both in transit and at rest, is a critical measure to ensure the confidentiality of information. Encryption guarantees that even if unauthorized access occurs, the data remains unintelligible. While cloud providers often offer encryption services, customers must appropriately manage encryption keys and access controls.

Effective Identity and Access Management (IAM) prevents unauthorized access to cloud resources. IAM practices, like role-based access control (or RBAC) and multi-factor authentication (MFA), ensure that access is granted only to authorized users with appropriate permissions. These measures reduce the risk of unauthorized access.

Cloud providers offer tools like security groups and network access control lists (NACLs) that allow organizations to define firewall rules and control traffic flow. Properly configured network controls limit exposure to potential threats and bolster the security of cloud resources.

Regular security assessments, which include vulnerability scanning and penetration testing, are crucial for identifying and addressing weaknesses in cloud configurations and applications. These assessments should be conducted periodically, especially after significant changes to cloud resources.

Compliance with the industry standards and the regulatory requirements is paramount, particularly in regulated industries like healthcare and finance. Conducting compliance audits ensures that an organization's security controls align with the necessary standards.

Security monitoring and incident response capabilities are essential for proactive threat detection and effective mitigation. Cloud environments generate extensive logs and telemetry data, necessitating the use of security information and event management (SIEM) solutions to aggregate and analyze this information. Furthermore, a well-defined incident response plan is crucial for swift and efficient responses to security incidents.

Cloud configuration management helps prevent misconfigurations, which are a common cause of cloud security incidents. Continuous monitoring and automation tools aid in identifying and rectifying misconfigurations promptly. Infrastructure as Code (IaC) practices enable organizations to define cloud resources with predefined security configurations, reducing the risk of human error.

Employee training and awareness are vital components of cloud security. One important contributing factor to security problems is still human error. Organizations should invest in comprehensive training and awareness programs to educate employees about cloud security best practices, potential risks, and how to report security incidents effectively.

Regular updates and patch management are essential to keep cloud resources, including virtual machines and cloud-based applications, up-to-date with security patches. Attackers can exploit vulnerabilities in outdated software.

In conclusion, cloud security best practices are essential for organizations leveraging cloud services to protect sensitive data and ensure the integrity of their cloud environments. These practices encompass understanding the shared responsibility model, data encryption, effective IAM, network controls, continuous security assessments, compliance audits, robust monitoring, incident response planning, cloud configuration management, employee training, and regular updates. Adhering to these best practices is essential as cloud adoption grows, enabling organizations to successfully navigate the evolving landscape of cloud security.

CHAPTER X

Mobile Security

Mobile device security

In an increasingly connected world, mobile devices are becoming a vital component of our daily lives since they facilitate communication, productivity, and easy access to a multitude of information. However, this pervasive use of mobile devices also makes them lucrative targets for cyberattacks, underscoring the critical importance of mobile device security. Protecting these devices is essential for individual users and organizations that rely on mobile technology for business operations.

One of the primary concerns in mobile device security is protecting sensitive data. Mobile devices often store a wealth of personal and business-related information, including emails, text messages, contact lists, and even financial data. To safeguard this information, encryption is a fundamental security measure. Data encryption ensures that even if a device is lost or stolen, the data remains inaccessible without the appropriate decryption key. Mobile operating systems, like iOS and Android, incorporate encryption features to protect data at rest and in transit.

Authentication and access control are essential components of mobile device security. Passwords, PINs, and biometric authentication methods like fingerprint recognition and facial recognition ensure that only authorized users can access the device. Multi-factor authentication (MFA) adds a further layer of security by requiring users to provide multiple verification forms.

Mobile app security is another crucial aspect of protecting mobile devices. The proliferation of mobile apps has created opportunities for malicious actors to exploit vulnerabilities. Users should download an application only from trusted sources, such as official app stores, to reduce the risk of downloading malicious software. App permissions, which dictate what data and features an app can access, should be reviewed and limited to the essentials. Developers must also follow secure coding practices to prevent vulnerabilities that attackers could exploit.

Regular software updates are vital for mobile device security. Manufacturers and operating system providers release updates that include security patches to address vulnerabilities. Keeping the device's software up-to-date ensures that these vulnerabilities are patched, reducing the risk of exploitation.

Mobile device management (MDM) solutions are valuable tools for organizations that manage fleets of mobile devices. MDM enables IT administrators to enforce security policies, remotely wipe devices in case of either loss or theft, and monitor device activity. These solutions are essential for organizations that allow employees to utilize personal devices for work-related tasks, known as BYOD (Bring Your Own Device) policies.

Secure communication is crucial when transmitting data between mobile devices, servers, or other devices. Transport Layer Security (TLS) and Virtual Private Networks (VPNs) are encryption protocols that protect data during transmission. Using secure communication methods is especially important when accessing sensitive information over public Wi-Fi networks, which are susceptible to eavesdropping by malicious actors.

Mobile device security also extends to physical protection. Users should be cautious about where and how they use their devices to prevent theft or unauthorized access. Enabling features like remote tracking and locking can help locate and secure a lost or stolen device. Moreover, enabling device encryption and strong authentication methods adds additional protection in case the device falls into the wrong hands.

In conclusion, mobile device security is critical in today's digital age. The widespread use of mobile devices and their capacity to store sensitive data makes them attractive targets for cybercriminals. Implementing robust security measures, like the data encryption, authentication, secure app practices, regular updates, and mobile device management solutions, is essential for safeguarding these devices and their information. As mobile technology continues to evolve and integrate into various aspects of our lives, the importance of mobile device security will only become more pronounced. It is incumbent upon individuals and organizations to prioritize and invest in mobile device security to protect their data and maintain the integrity of their digital activities.

Mobile app security

With its ability to perform an array of tasks, from interaction and entertainment to productivity and economics, mobile applications, or just mobile apps, have become a vital component of our everyday life. Still, there are a number of security issues that have arisen as a result of the widespread use of mobile apps. For the sake of safeguarding user information, privacy, and general digital health, mobile app security is crucial.

One of the primary security considerations for mobile apps is data protection. Mobile devices often store sensitive information such as personal messages, contact details, financial data, and even health records. To safeguard this data, mobile apps should implement robust encryption techniques. Encryption ensures that data is transformed into an unreadable format, making it inaccessible to unauthorized users even if they gain access to the device or the app's data storage.

Control of access and authentication are essential elements of mobile app security. Robust authentication methods, including passwords, PINs, biometric recognition (such as fingerprints or facial scans), and multi-factor authentication (MFA), help ensure that only authorized users can access the app's features and data. Properly designed access controls limit the privileges of different users and components within the app, preventing unauthorized access to sensitive functionalities.

Secure coding practices are paramount to preventing vulnerabilities in mobile apps. Developers must follow best practices to avoid common security pitfalls, such as input validation flaws, insecure data storage, and code injection vulnerabilities. Regular security testing, including code reviews and dynamic analysis, helps identify and remediate security issues during development.

App permissions are a critical aspect of mobile app security. Users are frequently asked to allow an app to access several device capabilities and data, like the camera, microphone, location, and contacts, when they install it. Users need to review and understand these permissions, as granting excessive or unnecessary permissions can compromise their privacy and security. Developers should also implement a principle of least privilege, requesting only the permissions necessary for the app's intended functionality.

Securing third-party components is another challenge in mobile app security. Many apps incorporate third-party libraries, frameworks, or services to add functionality or streamline development. However, these components can introduce security risks if not properly vetted and maintained. Developers should regularly update and patch third-party components to address known vulnerabilities.

Secure communication is essential for mobile apps that transmit data over networks. Transport Layer Security (TLS) is a widely used encryption protocol that ensures the confidentiality and integrity of data in transit. Mobile apps should implement TLS when communicating with remote servers to protect user data from eavesdropping and interception.

User education is a vital aspect of mobile app security. Users should know potential security risks, such as downloading apps from unofficial sources or clicking on suspicious links. Regularly updating apps on their devices is also crucial, as developers often release security patches to address vulnerabilities. Additionally, users should be cautious about granting app permissions and consider the necessity of each permission request.

Regular security assessments, like the penetration testing and vulnerability scanning, are essential to evaluate the security posture of mobile apps. These assessments help identify vulnerabilities that attackers could exploit and allow developers to remediate them promptly.

In conclusion, mobile app security is critical in the mobile-driven digital landscape. Mobile apps store and process sensitive data, making them attractive targets for cyberattacks. Implementing robust security measures, including data encryption, strong authentication, secure coding practices, proper permission management, third-party component security, and secure communication, is essential to protect user data and privacy. User education and awareness also play a pivotal role in maintaining mobile app security. As mobile technology evolves and shape our daily lives, the importance of mobile app security will only grow, making it imperative for developers and users alike to prioritize and invest in app security to guarantee the safety and integrity of the mobile app ecosystem.

BYOD policies and challenges

The initiation of Bring Your Own Device (BYOD) guidelines has changed how businesses handle workplace technology. Under the BYOD paradigm, workers utilize their own gadgets for work-related activities, including laptops, tablets, and cellphones. This strategy has many advantages, such as higher output and happier workers, but it also presents cybersecurity issues that companies need to resolve in order to safeguard confidential information and keep a safe online environment.

One of the primary challenges associated with BYOD policies is the diversity of devices and operating systems. Unlike traditional corporate-owned devices, which can be tightly controlled and standardized, BYOD environments feature a wide range of devices running various operating systems and software versions. This diversity complicates ensuring uniform security measures across all devices, making it challenging for IT teams to manage and secure them effectively.

Access control and authentication are essential elements of BYOD security. It becomes more difficult to make sure that only authorized users can access company resources when employees use their own devices for work. Securing sensitive data and verifying user identities require strong authentication techniques like multi-factor authentication (MFA). It can be difficult to deploy and enforce MFA on a variety of personal devices, though.

Data protection is another significant concern in BYOD environments. Personal devices often contain a mix of personal and corporate data, and maintaining separation between the two is crucial. Encryption plays a vital role in this regard, as it helps protect sensitive data, both in transit and at rest, regardless of whether it's on a personal or work-related application or device.

App security is a significant consideration in BYOD policies. Mobile apps, in particular, pose risks, as employees may download and use apps that haven't undergone thorough security assessments. Unsecure apps can introduce vulnerabilities or leak sensitive data. To mitigate this risk, organizations should implement app whitelisting and blacklisting, ensuring that only approved and secure apps can be used for work-related tasks.

Network security challenges also arise in BYOD environments. Devices connecting to corporate networks may not have the same security protections as corporate-owned devices. Malware or compromised devices can introduce threats into the network. Organizations should implement network segmentation and access controls to isolate personal devices from sensitive corporate resources.

Compliance and regulatory concerns are amplified in BYOD environments. Many industries are subject to rigorous data protection regulations, such as GDPR and HIPAA, which require organizations to safeguard sensitive data. Ensuring compliance with these regulations in a BYOD context can be complex, as organizations need to monitor and manage data across various personal devices.

Monitoring and incident response pose unique challenges in BYOD environments. Organizations must continuously monitor device activity for signs of suspicious behavior or security incidents. Additionally, incident response plans must be tailored to address potential BYOD-specific threats, such as data breaches on personal devices or the loss of a device containing sensitive corporate data.

User education and awareness are critical in BYOD policies. Employees must be informed about the risks associated with using personal devices for work and trained on security best practices. This includes understanding the importance of regular updates, strong passwords, and safe app usage.

In conclusion, BYOD policies offer undeniable advantages in flexibility and employee satisfaction, but they also bring complex cybersecurity challenges. Organizations must balance enabling employees to use their personal devices for work and implementing robust security measures to protect sensitive data. Overcoming the challenges of BYOD policies requires a multifaceted approach, including strong authentication, data protection, app security, network security, compliance adherence, monitoring, incident response, and user education. Successfully navigating these challenges allows organizations to harness the benefits of BYOD policies while safeguarding their digital assets in an evolving cybersecurity landscape.

CHAPTER XI

Social Engineering and Phishing Attacks

Understanding social engineering attacks

Social engineering attacks represent a category of cyber threats that manipulate human psychology rather than exploit technical vulnerabilities. These attacks aim to deceive individuals or organizations into divulging confidential information, performing specific actions, or providing unauthorized access. Understanding social engineering attacks is crucial for individuals and organizations alike, as they continue to be a prevalent and effective method cyber criminals use.

One of the most common forms of social engineering attacks is phishing. Phishing emails or messages impersonate legitimate entities, such as banks, government agencies, or trusted brands, to trick recipients into disclosing sensitive information like passwords, credit card numbers, or personal identification. Phishing emails often contain urgent or alarming language to create a sense of urgency, compelling recipients to act quickly without thinking critically.

Spear phishing is a more targeted variation of phishing where attackers customize their messages for specific individuals or organizations. By researching their targets and using personal information, attackers can create convincing messages that appear legitimate. This attack is often used in corporate espionage or to access high-value accounts.

Another variant of social engineering attacks is pretexting, which involves creating a fabricated scenario or pretext to manipulate individuals into providing information or performing actions they wouldn't under normal circumstances. For instance, an attacker might pose as a company's IT support and request login credentials from an employee to "resolve a technical issue."

Baiting is a social engineering attack that entails offering something enticing, such as free software or media downloads, to lure victims into a trap. When victims click on the bait, they unknowingly download malicious software onto their devices. This type of attack can lead to the compromise of sensitive information or the installation of malware.

Tailgating, or piggybacking, occurs when an attacker obtains physical access to a restricted area by following an authorized person without their knowledge. This method is often used to infiltrate secure buildings or facilities. Attackers may pose as delivery personnel, maintenance workers, or employees to bypass security measures.

Preventing social engineering attacks demands a combination of cybersecurity measures and user awareness. Organizations should implement robust email filtering and authentication mechanisms to detect and block phishing attempts. Multi-factor authentication (MFA) should be enforced to add layer of user accounts security, making it challenging for attackers to obtain unauthorized access.

User education is a crucial aspect of defense against social engineering attacks. Employees should be trained to recognize common social engineering tactics, such as suspicious emails, pretexting attempts, or unsolicited requests for sensitive information. Awareness training can help individuals develop a healthy skepticism and encourage them to verify requests from unknown or unexpected sources.

In addition to training, individuals should practice good password hygiene by using strong, unique passwords for each account and changing them regularly. They should also be cautious when clicking links or downloading files, especially from unknown sources.

Security awareness is not limited to employees; it also extends to individuals in their personal lives. Protecting personal information, securing home networks, and being cautious about sharing sensitive details on social media platforms can help mitigate the risk of social engineering attacks targeting individuals.

In conclusion, social engineering attacks continue to be a significant threat in the ever-evolving landscape of cybersecurity. These attacks prey on human psychology and deception, making them difficult to prevent solely with technical measures. To effectively defend against social engineering attacks, cybersecurity technology, user education, and awareness are necessary. By understanding the various tactics used in social engineering attacks and practicing vigilance in professional and personal contexts, individuals and organizations can reduce the risk of falling victim to these deceptive and damaging attacks.

Phishing techniques and prevention

Phishing is a widespread and highly effective form of cyberattack that targets individuals, organizations, and even governments. It involves fraudulent attempts to deceive individuals into revealing sensitive information, like the passwords, credit card numbers, or personal identification. Phishing techniques have evolved significantly, becoming more sophisticated and challenging to detect. Understanding these techniques and implementing prevention measures is essential to protect against phishing attacks.

One common phishing technique is email phishing. Attackers send deceptive emails that appear to be from legitimate sources, like the banks, government agencies, or well-known brands. These emails often contain urgent or threatening language, designed to create a sense of urgency or fear, compelling recipients to take immediate action. Usually, the activity is clicking on a malicious link which directs users to a fake website intended to steal personal data, such as login credentials. In order to prevent email phishing, users should be taught to be wary of unsolicited emails, to double-check the sender's identity, and to stay away from suspicious links.

Spear phishing is a highly focused form of phishing that involves tailored assaults directed at particular people or companies. Attackers research their targets to craft personalized messages, often using information gathered from social media or public sources. These messages may appear highly convincing, making it difficult for recipients to discern the malicious intent. Prevention strategies for spear phishing include user awareness training, strong email authentication, and the implementation of advanced threat detection tools that can identify suspicious email patterns and behaviors.

Voice phishing, or vishing, is a phishing technique that involves phone calls or voice messages. Attackers often impersonate legitimate entities, such as bank representatives or tech support personnel, to trick victims into revealing sensitive information over the phone. Vishing can be challenging to detect because attackers use voice manipulation techniques to sound convincing. Prevention measures include verifying the caller's identity, not sharing sensitive information over the phone unless the user initiates the call, and reporting suspicious calls to authorities.

Smishing, or SMS phishing, is a phishing technique that targets individuals through text messages. Attackers send fraudulent SMS messages containing links or instructions that lead to phishing websites or malware downloads. These messages often appear as urgent notifications or offers. Preventing smishing attacks involves educating users to be aware about clicking on links in text messages, verifying the sender's identity, and not sharing sensitive information via SMS.

Prevention strategies for phishing attacks involve a combination of technology and user education. Email filtering solutions can help detect and block phishing emails before they reach users' inboxes. Multi-factor authentication (MFA) should be implemented to add a further layer of security to user accounts, making it more difficult for attackers to obtain unauthorized access. User awareness training is a critical prevention component, as it empowers individuals to recognize phishing attempts and respond appropriately. Regular phishing simulations can help organizations assess their employees' preparedness and improve their defenses.

Additionally, organizations should implement robust email authentication mechanisms, like Domain-based Message Authentication, Reporting, and Conformance, abbreviated as DMARC, to prevent email spoofing and domain impersonation. Advanced threat detection tools that use machine learning and behavioral analysis can help identify and mitigate phishing attempts in real time. Users should be encouraged to promptly report suspected phishing emails to IT or security teams.

In conclusion, phishing attacks are still a common and developing issue in the field of cybersecurity. Attackers employ various techniques to deceive individuals and organizations, from email phishing to vishing and smishing. Preventing phishing attacks requires a multifaceted approach that combines technological defenses, user education, and ongoing awareness efforts. By understanding the techniques employed in phishing attacks and implementing robust prevention measures, individuals and organizations can reduce their susceptibility to these deceptive and damaging cyberattacks.

Social engineering awareness and training

Social engineering attacks continue to be a pervasive and significant threat to individuals and organizations. These attacks rely on manipulating human psychology to deceive individuals into disclosing sensitive information or performing actions compromising security. Given the sophistication and diversity of social engineering techniques, raising awareness and providing training to individuals is crucial in defending against these deceptive tactics.

Awareness of social engineering attacks begins with recognizing the attackers' various tactics. Phishing, for instance, involves fraudulent emails or messages that impersonate trusted entities to trick recipients into revealing sensitive information. Individuals should be educated on the typical red flags of phishing emails, such as unexpected urgency, unfamiliar senders, and suspicious URLs, to help them identify potential threats.

A highly focused type of phishing known as spear phishing uses tailored attacks directed at certain people or companies. Attackers often gather information from social media or public sources to craft convincing messages. Individuals need to understand that attackers may use seemingly legitimate information to deceive them. Training should emphasize the importance of verifying sender identities and being cautious about sharing sensitive information, even in seemingly legitimate communications.

Vishing, or voice phishing, involves deceptive phone calls or voice messages in which attackers impersonate trusted entities to extract sensitive information. Individuals should be educated to verify the identity of callers and refrain from sharing sensitive data over the phone, especially in unsolicited calls. Reporting suspicious calls to authorities is an essential step in addressing vishing attempts.

Smishing, or SMS phishing, targets individuals through text messages that contain malicious links or instructions. These messages often appear as urgent notifications or enticing offers. Social engineering awareness should extend to recognizing the dangers of clicking on links in text messages and verifying the sender's identity before taking any action.

Social engineering attacks also occur in physical settings. Tailgating, for example, involves an attacker gaining unauthorized access to a secure area by following an authorized individual. Employees should be trained to challenge and report unfamiliar individuals attempting to enter secure premises.

User education is a critical component of social engineering awareness and training. Individuals should be made aware of the potential risks and consequences of falling victim to these attacks. Training programs should include practical exercises, such as simulated phishing campaigns, to help individuals recognize and respond to social engineering attempts effectively.

Additionally, organizations can implement security policies and best practices to reinforce social engineering awareness. These policies should cover data protection, access controls, and incident reporting. Regular security updates and reminders can help keep social engineering awareness at the forefront of employees' minds.

Collaboration between security teams and employees is essential in maintaining social engineering awareness. Employees should feel comfortable reporting suspicious activities or incidents to the appropriate authorities. Clear reporting procedures and a non-punitive approach can encourage employees to proactively address potential threats.

In conclusion, social engineering awareness and training are essential components of cybersecurity defense in today's digital landscape. Social engineering attacks are diverse and deceptive, making it critical for individuals and organizations to be vigilant and well-prepared. Recognizing the various tactics employed in social engineering, from phishing and spear phishing to vishing, smishing, and physical attacks like tailgating, is the first step in defense. Effective training programs that raise awareness and educate individuals on recognizing and responding to these threats can significantly enhance an organization's security posture. Social engineering attackers use deceptive techniques, and individuals and organizations can strengthen their defenses against them by cultivating a culture of security awareness and ongoing learning.

CHAPTER XII

Incident Response and Disaster Recovery

Preparing for incidents

It's a frightening fact that cybersecurity incidents are inevitable in today's digital environment. Organizations can suffer greatly from cyberattacks and data breaches, which can lead to everything from financial losses and reputational harm to legal issues and mistrust from customers. As such, businesses must adopt a proactive approach to cybersecurity by preparing for incidents. Incident preparedness involves a series of strategic and tactical measures to minimize the impact of security breaches and respond effectively when they occur.

One of the fundamental elements of incident preparedness is developing an incident response plan (IRP). An IRP is a structured framework that outlines the steps an organization should implement in the event of a cybersecurity incident. It includes procedures for identifying, containing, mitigating, and recovering from incidents. An effective IRP should be tailored to the organization's specific needs and regularly updated to address evolving threats and technologies.

Incident response teams play a pivotal role in the execution of an IRP. These teams consist of professionals with expertise in various areas of cybersecurity, including forensics, legal, communication, and technical remediation. The incident response team's responsibilities encompass investigating incidents, preserving evidence, coordinating with relevant authorities, and restoring normal operations. The team's composition and responsibilities should be clearly defined in the IRP.

Another critical component of incident preparedness is employee training and awareness. Employees are often the first line of defense against cybersecurity threats, and their ability to recognize and report suspicious activities is invaluable. Regular cybersecurity training programs can educate employees about common attack vectors, such as phishing, and help them understand their roles and responsibilities in incident response.

Continuous monitoring and threat intelligence are essential for early incident detection. Organizations should implement robust security monitoring solutions that can identify anomalous behavior and potential indicators of compromise. Threat intelligence feeds provide valuable insights into emerging threats and attack trends, enabling organizations to adjust their security measures proactively.

Data backup and recovery plans are essential for ensuring business continuity during a cybersecurity incident. Regular data backups, both onsite and offsite, help organizations recover from data loss caused by incidents like ransomware attacks. Testing the restoration process is equally crucial to verify the effectiveness of backup and recovery procedures.

Intrusion detection and prevention systems (IDPS) are instrumental in identifying and blocking malicious activities in real time. These systems can help organizations detect and respond to incidents swiftly, reducing the impact of an attack. Implementing robust access controls and least privilege principles further limits the exposure of critical systems and data, making it harder for attackers to move laterally within the network.

Legal and regulatory considerations are vital aspects of incident preparedness. Organizations must know their jurisdiction, the industry's legal obligations, and reporting requirements for cybersecurity incidents. Engaging legal counsel with expertise in cybersecurity can help organizations navigate the complex legal landscape associated with incidents.

Effective communication is paramount during incident response. Establishing communication protocols and designated spokespeople ensures accurate and timely information is disseminated to stakeholders, including employees, customers, partners, and regulatory authorities. Transparent communication can help mitigate reputational damage and maintain trust.

Lastly, organizations should conduct tabletop exercises and incident simulations regularly. These exercises test the effectiveness of the IRP, the incident response team's capabilities, and the organization's overall preparedness. Lessons learned from these exercises should inform improvements to the IRP and the broader cybersecurity strategy.

In conclusion, preparing for cybersecurity incidents is not a matter of if but when. A proactive and well-structured incident preparedness strategy is essential for reducing the impact of incidents and ensuring a swift and effective response. This strategy encompasses incident response planning, dedicated response teams, employee training, continuous monitoring, data backup, legal considerations, and communication protocols. By investing in incident preparedness, organizations can enhance their cybersecurity posture and better protect their data, reputation, and overall resilience in the face of cyber threats.

Incident response planning and execution

In today's hyperconnected digital landscape, the certainty of cybersecurity incidents demands a proactive and well-structured approach to incident response. An effective incident response plan (IRP) is a cornerstone of an organization's cybersecurity strategy, providing a structured framework for identifying, containing, mitigating, and recovering from incidents. The successful execution of this plan is paramount for minimizing the impact of incidents, safeguarding sensitive data, and ensuring business continuity.

The initial step in incident response planning is recognizing the need for a comprehensive IRP. Organizations must acknowledge that cybersecurity incidents are not a matter of if, but when. This recognition forms the basis for proactive planning and investment in incident response capabilities. Once an organization commits to incident response preparedness, it can begin the process of developing and implementing an IRP.

The development of an IRP involves a series of strategic and tactical considerations. The plan should outline the roles and responsibilities of an incident response team, which consists of experts in various facets of cybersecurity, including forensics, legal, communication, and technical remediation. Clear delineation of team members' roles and responsibilities is crucial for an effective response. It ensures that the right individuals are mobilized to address specific aspects of an incident, from technical analysis to legal compliance.

Another vital aspect of IRP development is the establishment of incident categories and severity levels. Incidents can vary widely in terms of impact and scope, ranging from minor security breaches to significant data breaches or system compromises. Categorizing incidents and assigning severity levels helps organizations prioritize their response efforts. It enables teams to allocate resources effectively based on each incident's perceived risk and impact.

IRPs should also define the steps and procedures for incident detection, containment, eradication, and recovery. This includes guidelines for preserving evidence, coordinating with relevant authorities, restoring normal operations, and communicating with stakeholders. The plan should be customized to the organization's specific needs and regularly updated to reflect changes in technology, threats, and regulatory requirements.

When an incident occurs, the execution of the IRP becomes paramount. Incident response teams must act swiftly and decisively to limit the damage and minimize downtime. The first step is often detection, which involves identifying indicators of compromise (IOCs) and signs of an incident. Continuous monitoring, intrusion detection systems, and threat intelligence feeds are critical in early incident detection.

Once an incident is detected, containment efforts begin. This may involve isolating affected systems or networks to prevent further spread of the incident. The goal is to minimize the impact while maintaining the integrity of potential evidence. During this phase, forensics experts may gather data and analyze the incident to fully understand its scope and impact.

Eradication involves identifying the root cause of the incident and eliminating it. This phase may require patching vulnerabilities, removing malware, or reconfiguring compromised systems. Simultaneously, the incident response team collaborates with legal counsel to guarantee compliance with regulatory requirements and reporting obligations.

The recovery phase focuses on restoring normal operations. Data recovery, system restoration, and stakeholder communication are critical aspects of this phase. Organizations should have documented procedures and checklists to expedite the recovery process.

Communication is a vital thread running through every phase of incident response. Clear and transparent communication with internal and external stakeholders is essential. Designated spokespeople should provide updates and information to employees, customers, partners, and regulatory authorities. Transparent communication helps maintain trust, manage reputational damage, and ensure a coordinated response effort.

Finally, post-incident analysis, or lessons learned, is critical to incident response. After an incident is resolved, organizations should conduct a thorough analysis to understand what went well and what can be improved. These insights inform updates to the IRP, security measures, and employee training.

In conclusion, incident response planning and execution are essential components of an organization's cybersecurity strategy. The development of a well-structured IRP, the proactive training of an incident response team, and the timely execution of the plan are critical for minimizing the impact of incidents and ensuring business continuity. The ability to detect, contain, eradicate, and recover from incidents swiftly and effectively is crucial in safeguarding sensitive data, maintaining trust, and mitigating the evolving threats in the digital age.

Disaster recovery strategies

In cybersecurity and IT management, disaster recovery strategies are essential safeguards that organizations implement to ensure the continuity of their operations in the face of unexpected and potentially catastrophic events. These strategies encompass a range of measures and practices designed to minimize downtime, protect critical data, and facilitate the rapid restoration of IT systems following disasters, whether natural disasters, cyberattacks, or other unforeseen events. Disaster recovery strategies are crucial to an organization's overall business continuity planning.

One of the primary elements of disaster recovery strategies is the creation of comprehensive and well-documented disaster recovery plans (DRPs). These plans provide a roadmap for how an organization will respond during a disaster. DRPs typically include detailed procedures for data backup, system restoration, and communication, as well as roles and responsibilities for disaster recovery team members. Developing and regularly updating these plans is critical to ensuring they remain effective and relevant in the face of evolving threats and technologies.

Data backup and recovery are foundational components of disaster recovery strategies. Organizations should establish robust and redundant backup systems to ensure the security and accessibility of critical data. This often involves regularly copying data to offsite locations or cloud-based storage, ensuring that data can be restored even if the primary data center is compromised. The frequency of backups and retention policies should align with the organization's recovery time objectives (RTOs) and recovery point objectives (RPOs), which define how quickly data needs to be restored and how much data loss is acceptable.

Virtualization technology plays a significant role in disaster recovery. Organizations can minimize downtime and expedite the recovery process by creating virtual replicas of physical systems and applications. In the event of a disaster, these virtualized systems can be brought online quickly, reducing the impact on business operations. Additionally, organizations should consider using failover mechanisms that automatically redirect traffic to backup systems when primary systems are unavailable.

Cloud computing has revolutionized disaster recovery strategies. Cloud-based disaster recovery as a service (DRaaS) providers offer scalable and cost-effective data storage, backup, and recovery solutions. Organizations can leverage the cloud to replicate critical systems and data, providing high resilience. Cloud-based solutions also offer the advantage of geographic diversity, allowing data to be stored in multiple regions to mitigate risks associated with regional disasters.

Testing and simulation are essential components of disaster recovery strategies. Organizations should regularly conduct disaster recovery drills and exercises to validate the effectiveness of their plans and processes. These tests help identify weaknesses and areas for improvement, ensuring that the organization can respond swiftly and effectively when a real disaster occurs. In addition to full-scale tests, smaller-scale tests, such as data recovery tests and tabletop exercises, can also be valuable in assessing readiness.

Security considerations are paramount in disaster recovery. Organizations must ensure that backup and recovery processes do not introduce vulnerabilities that cybercriminals could exploit. Encryption, access controls, and authentication mechanisms should be in place to protect data both in transit and at rest during the recovery process.

Regulatory compliance is another critical aspect of disaster recovery strategies. Many industries have specific regulations and requirements regarding data retention and disaster recovery. Organizations must ensure that their disaster recovery plans align with these regulations and can demonstrate compliance to auditors and regulatory authorities.

In conclusion, disaster recovery strategies are integral to modern business continuity planning. Organizations can enhance their resilience by developing comprehensive disaster recovery plans, implementing robust data backup and recovery processes, leveraging virtualization and cloud technologies, conducting regular testing and simulation, addressing security concerns, and ensuring regulatory compliance. These strategies protect critical data and safeguard the organization's reputation and operations, ensuring that it can continue to thrive despite unforeseen events.

CHAPTER XIII

Legal and Ethical Aspects of Hacking

Legal implications of hacking

Unauthorized entry to or manipulation of computer systems and data, or "hacking," carries significant legal implications and can have severe repercussions for those who engage in it. While country-specific laws pertaining to hacking differ, there are global patterns that handle this cybersecurity concern. Understanding the legal implications of hacking is essential for individuals and organizations as they navigate the complex landscape of cybercrime and cybersecurity enforcement.

Hacking may violate laws pertaining to computer crime, which is one of the biggest legal repercussions. Unauthorized access to computer systems is strictly prohibited and may result in criminal penalties in many jurisdictions. Charges for data theft, computer fraud, illegal access, and the distribution of malicious software may be brought against hackers. The seriousness of the offense and the harm imposed can determine the length of prison sentences and large fines associated with a conviction under these laws.

Intellectual property theft is another critical legal issue associated with hacking. Hackers may target businesses and organizations to steal proprietary information, trade secrets, or intellectual property. These thefts can lead to civil lawsuits and substantial financial damages for the hackers and the organizations affected. Intellectual property theft can harm a company's competitive advantage and lead to significant legal disputes over ownership and damages.

Privacy violations are a prevalent legal concern in hacking cases. Hackers often access personal information without consent, such as financial records, medical records, or personal emails. To secure individuals' personal data, organizations must abide by strict privacy regulations, such as Health Insurance Portability and Accountability Act, abbreviated as HIPAA, of the United States and the General Data Protection Regulation (GDPR) of the European Union. Hacking incidents that reveal private information about a person may lead to fines from the authorities, legal action, and reputational harm to the company.

Common hacking techniques like Distributed Denial of Service (DDoS) involve flooding a target's computer system or network with excessive traffic that it becomes inaccessible. DDoS attacks can disrupt essential services and cause financial losses to organizations. Engaging in or orchestrating DDoS attacks is illegal in most jurisdictions and can lead to criminal charges and significant penalties.

Cyberextortion is a growing threat associated with hacking. Hackers may deploy ransomware to encrypt an organization's data, demanding a ransom for its release. Paying a ransom may be illegal in some jurisdictions, and organizations that fall victim to cyber extortion may still face legal consequences. Additionally, even if the ransom is paid, the hacker is not guaranteed to honor their end of the bargain.

Hacking cases become more complex due to international legal issues. Since hackers frequently work beyond national borders, it can be difficult for law authorities to find and bring them to justice. International cooperation and treaties, such as the Budapest Convention on Cybercrime, facilitate efforts to combat cybercrime across jurisdictions. However, legal challenges related to jurisdiction and extradition can complicate prosecuting hackers operating in countries with lax cybersecurity enforcement.

Hacking can also have indirect legal implications for organizations. Regulatory bodies, like Securities and Exchange Commission (or SEC) of U.S. or the Information Commissioner's Office (ICO) in the UK, may impose fines on organizations that fail to protect their systems adequately. Shareholders and customers affected by data breaches may also initiate lawsuits against organizations for negligence or inadequate security measures.

In conclusion, the legal implications of hacking are extensive and far-reaching. Hacking activities can result in criminal charges, civil lawsuits, regulatory fines, and damage to an individual's or organization's reputation. As the global legal landscape surrounding cybersecurity continues to evolve, individuals and organizations must prioritize cybersecurity measures, follow legal requirements, and stay informed about the latest legal developments related to hacking to mitigate the risks associated with this pervasive cybercrime.

Ethical considerations for ethical hackers

Penetration testing, white hat hacking, and ethical hacking are terms for the deliberate probing of computer systems, networks, and applications to find flaws and vulnerabilities. Professionals in cybersecurity or penetration testing, commonly referred to as ethical hackers, are essential in assisting companies in strengthening their security stance. However, ethical hacking is not without ethical considerations and responsibilities. Ethical hackers must adhere to ethical guidelines to ensure their actions are legal and morally sound.

One of the foremost ethical considerations for ethical hackers is obtaining proper authorization. Unauthorized hacking or penetration testing can have severe legal consequences, as it may be considered a breach of computer crime laws. Ethical hackers must always seek written permission from the organization or system owner before conducting any testing. This authorization should specify the testing's scope, objectives, and limitations to ensure that the ethical hacker's actions remain within legal boundaries.

Transparency is another vital ethical principle for ethical hackers. They should clearly communicate their intentions to the organization they are testing and avoid any actions that may cause unnecessary panic or disruption. Ethical hackers must be forthcoming about their activities, explaining their methodologies and sharing findings with the organization's stakeholders. Open and honest communication fosters trust between the ethical hacker and the organization, which is essential for a successful collaboration.

Respecting privacy is a fundamental ethical consideration. Ethical hackers must ensure they do not violate individuals' or employees' privacy rights during testing. This means avoiding the collection or exposure of sensitive personal information that is not directly related to the security assessment. Ethical hackers should identify vulnerabilities and weaknesses rather than prying into personal data.

Informed consent is critical when conducting ethical hacking activities. Organizations must obtain permission from individuals affected by the testing, especially if it involves systems or networks used by employees or customers. Ethical hackers should ensure that their actions do not disrupt or harm individuals' access to essential services or their personal data.

Confidentiality is another ethical principle that ethical hackers must uphold. They are often privy to sensitive information about an organization's security posture, vulnerabilities, and potential weaknesses. It is the ethical responsibility of ethical hackers to safeguard this data from illegal access and to keep it private. Breaching confidentiality can harm an organization's reputation and security.

The principle of responsible disclosure is essential in the ethical hacking community. Ethical hackers who identify vulnerabilities must report their findings to the organization promptly. They should also provide adequate time for the organization to address the issues before disclosing them publicly. Responsible disclosure allows organizations to patch vulnerabilities and protect their systems, minimizing the risk of exploitation by malicious hackers.

Continual learning and improvement are ethical imperatives for ethical hackers. The field of cybersecurity is dynamic, with new threats and vulnerabilities emerging regularly. Ethical hackers must invest in ongoing education and stay updated with the most recent techniques, tools, and best practices. This commitment to knowledge and skill development ensures that ethical hackers can assist organizations most effectively.

Maintaining objectivity and impartiality is crucial for ethical hackers. Their primary responsibility is objectively identifying vulnerabilities and weaknesses, without bias or preconceived notions. They should avoid conflicts of interest that could compromise their impartiality and the integrity of their assessments.

In conclusion, ethical considerations are integral to the practice of ethical hacking. Ethical hackers play a vital role in helping organizations secure their digital assets, but they must do so with a strong commitment to ethical principles. Obtaining proper authorization, transparency, privacy protection, informed consent, confidentiality, responsible disclosure, continual learning, objectivity, and impartiality are all essential ethical considerations that guide the actions of ethical hackers. Ethical hackers can contribute to a safer digital world by adhering to these principles while maintaining the highest standards of ethics and professionalism.

Laws and regulations governing hacking

Hacking, the unauthorized access, manipulation, or compromise of computer systems, networks, and data, has become a global concern due to the increasing frequency and sophistication of cyberattacks. Governments worldwide have implemented a complex web of laws and regulations governing hacking to combat this threat and maintain the integrity of digital systems. These laws aim to define what constitutes illegal hacking, establish penalties for offenders, and provide a framework for prosecuting cybercriminals. Understanding these legal frameworks is crucial for individuals and organizations to navigate the legal landscape surrounding hacking.

One of the fundamental aspects of hacking laws is the classification of hacking activities. Laws typically distinguish between different categories of hacking based on intent and impact. Unauthorized entry to computer systems, networks, or data without malicious intent may be treated differently than hacking activities with malicious intent, such as data theft, fraud, or cyber espionage. Some legal systems also consider the severity of harm caused, financial losses incurred, or whether hacking activities targeted critical infrastructure or government systems.

Many countries have specific computer crime laws that address hacking. In the United States, for instance, the Computer Fraud and Abuse Act (CFAA) criminalizes various hacking activities, such as unauthorized access to protected computer systems, the transmission of malicious code, and identity theft. CFAA penalties can vary according on the seriousness of the offense, from fines to lengthy prison time.

In the European Union, the Cybercrime Directive and member states' national laws provide a legal framework for addressing hacking activities. These laws harmonize regulations across the EU and establish consistent definitions of cybercrimes. Offenders can face significant penalties, including fines and imprisonment.

Additionally, international treaties and agreements play a crucial role in governing hacking activities. The Budapest Convention on Cybercrime is one such treaty that facilitates international cooperation in combatting cybercrime, including hacking. Signatory countries agree to harmonize their legal frameworks, streamline investigations, and assist each other in prosecuting cybercriminals.

The legal landscape surrounding hacking extends beyond criminal penalties to include civil liability. Individuals and organizations affected by hacking incidents often have the right to seek compensation or damages through civil lawsuits. Victims may sue hackers for financial losses, data breaches, or other harms resulting from hacking activities.

Privacy laws are closely intertwined with hacking regulations. Numerous nations have passed data protection legislation, like the California Consumer Privacy Act (or CCPA) in the US and the General Data Protection Regulation (or GDPR) in the EU, mandating that businesses protect the personal data of their clients. Unauthorized access or data breaches resulting from hacking activities can lead to substantial fines and legal consequences under these privacy laws.

Moreover, regulations governing hacking extend to critical infrastructure and government systems. Hacking attempts against infrastructure like power grids, water treatment plants, or financial systems are treated with the utmost seriousness due to the potential for significant societal harm. Governments have implemented stringent regulations to protect these critical systems and ensure their resilience against cyberattacks.

In conclusion, the legal framework surrounding hacking is multifaceted and continually evolving to address the evolving landscape of cyber threats. These laws and regulations aim to define hacking activities, establish penalties for offenders, and provide a means for prosecuting cybercriminals. They also reflect the international nature of cybercrime, with treaties and agreements facilitating cross-border cooperation in combatting hacking and other cybercrimes. Understanding the legal implications of hacking is essential for individuals and organizations to navigate this complex terrain and ensure compliance with the law while safeguarding their digital assets.

CHAPTER XIV

Emerging Trends in Cybersecurity

Current and future trends in cybersecurity

Because of the rapid pace at which technology is developing and the continuously shifting strategies used by cybercriminals, the field of cybersecurity is always changing. Staying ahead of emerging threats and adopting innovative security measures are paramount for individuals, organizations, and governments. Here, we explore current and future cybersecurity trends, shedding light on the challenges as well as opportunities that lie ahead.

Because of their capacity to identify and react to threats instantly, artificial intelligence (also called AI) and machine learning, also called ML, have become more important in the field of cybersecurity. Large-scale statistics are analyzed by AI-driven systems to find trends and abnormalities that could be signs of cyberattacks. By automating threat detection, they can facilitate quicker reaction times and lighten the burden on security employees. Cybercriminals, however, also use AI to launch more complex attacks, which fuels a continuous arms race in the cybersecurity industry.

A security paradigm called Zero Trust Architecture makes the assumption that no entity, whether within or external to the company, can be trusted by default. Instead, every user and device attempting to access network resources must undergo verification and ongoing authentication. In the age of cloud computing and remote work, where traditional perimeter-based security measures are insufficient, this architecture provides increased protection.

Since cloud services are being used extensively, protecting cloud environments has taken on greater importance. Stricter access controls, the use of cloud-native security solutions, and the use of DevSecOps techniques to incorporate security throughout the whole software development lifecycle are examples of current developments in cloud security.

The proliferation of IoT devices introduces new security challenges. These devices often lack robust security features, making them susceptible to exploitation. IoT security trends include improved device authentication, encryption, and network segmentation to protect against potential threats.

Quantum computing has the capacity to break current encryption algorithms, posing a significant threat to data security. To counter this, researchers are developing quantum-resistant encryption methods, ensuring that data remains secure even in a world with powerful quantum computers.

Ransomware attacks have surged in recent years, with cybercriminals encrypting data and demanding ransoms for its release. Future trends in ransomware prevention involve robust backup and recovery strategies and improving user education to recognize phishing attempts.

Attackers increasingly target organizations' supply chains, compromising software or hardware during development or distribution. Strengthening supply chain security involves rigorous vetting of suppliers, software integrity checks, and secure update processes.

Governments worldwide are enacting stricter data protection laws and regulations. Staying compliant is a legal requirement and a means of enhancing cybersecurity. Privacy by design, data minimization, and transparent data practices are vital elements in compliance efforts.

Recognizing that humans are often the weakest link in cybersecurity, organizations invest in security awareness training and human-centric security measures. This includes multi-factor authentication, behavioral analytics, and zero-trust policies.

The future of cybersecurity may see the rise of autonomous security systems that can detect, respond to, and mitigate threats without human intervention. These systems will rely heavily on AI and ML for real-time threat analysis and response.

In conclusion, the current and future cybersecurity trends reflect the field's dynamic nature. While emerging technologies like AI and cloud computing offer innovative solutions, they also present new challenges and risks. Cybersecurity professionals must remain vigilant, adapt to evolving threats, and embrace a proactive approach to protect against cyberattacks. As the digital landscape continues to grow, staying informed about these trends and adopting best practices is crucial for individuals as well as organizations to make sure their digital assets remain secure and resilient in the face of emerging threats.

Artificial intelligence and machine learning in cybersecurity

Artificial intelligence (also called AI) and machine learning, also called ML, are revolutionizing the field of cybersecurity, offering new ways to detect, prevent, and respond to cyber threats. As the digital landscape becomes more and more complex and cyberattacks grow in sophistication, the capabilities of AI and ML are indispensable for staying ahead of cybercriminals. In this section, we explore the role of AI and ML in cybersecurity, their applications, and the benefits they bring to the ongoing battle against cyber threats.

AI and ML have emerged as potent tools in the realm of cybersecurity due to their ability to analyze vast datasets, recognize patterns, and make intelligent decisions in real-time. One of their primary applications is in threat detection and analysis. AI-powered security systems can continuously monitor network traffic, user behavior, and system activities to identify anomalies and potential threats. Early threat detection is made possible by machine learning algorithms that may be trained to differentiate between normal and malevolent activity using past data.

Moreover, AI and ML enhance the accuracy and efficiency of threat detection by reducing false positives. Traditional rule-based systems often generate numerous false alarms, overwhelming security teams and leading to alert fatigue. AI can refine the analysis of security alerts by considering context, user behavior, and known attack patterns, enabling security teams to focus on the most critical threats.

Another crucial role of AI and ML in cybersecurity is identifying previously unknown threats. Cybercriminals constantly develop new attack techniques and malware variants that evade traditional signature-based security measures. ML models can identify zero-day threats by recognizing deviations from established baselines, even if the threat has not been seen before. This proactive approach is essential in an environment where threat landscapes constantly evolve.

AI and ML also play a pivotal role in automating incident response. When a security breach occurs, rapid response is critical to minimize damage. AI-driven security systems can autonomously analyze the scope and severity of an incident, assess potential impact, and initiate appropriate response actions. This automation accelerates incident containment and reduces the time it takes to mitigate threats.

Access control and authentication are improved by AI and ML in addition to threat identification and response. Multi-factor authentication systems powered by AI can adapt to users' behavior and adjust authentication requirements accordingly. This dynamic approach strengthens security while providing a seamless user experience.

Furthermore, AI and ML assist in fraud prevention and detection in various sectors, including finance and e-commerce. These technologies analyze transaction patterns, user behavior, and historical data to identify fraudulent activities, preventing financial losses and safeguarding customer trust.

The benefits of AI and ML in cybersecurity are substantial, but they are not without challenges. One significant challenge is the potential for adversarial attacks, where cybercriminals manipulate AI systems to evade detection.

Researchers are actively developing robust AI models that are resilient to such attacks.

Another challenge is the need for large datasets to train ML models effectively. Quality data is crucial for building accurate models, and organizations must ensure data privacy and compliance with regulations when collecting and using this data.

In conclusion, AI and ML are reshaping the cybersecurity landscape. They bring sophisticated threat detection, proactive identification of unknown threats, streamlined incident response, and enhanced access control. While challenges exist, the benefits of AI and ML in cybersecurity far outweigh the drawbacks. As the digital world continues to evolve, the role of AI and ML in cybersecurity will only become more central in protecting organizations and individuals from an ever-expanding array of cyber threats.

Quantum computing and its impact on encryption

The advent of quantum computing represents a monumental shift in the world of technology and has significant implications for various domains, including cybersecurity. Quantum computers have the capacity to perform complex calculations at speeds that are currently inconceivable by classical computers. While this promises tremendous advancements in many fields, it also poses a considerable threat to traditional encryption methods that underpin the security of our digital world. In this section, we delve into quantum computing, explore its impact on encryption in cybersecurity, and examine the strategies and solutions developed to address this emerging challenge.

To comprehend the impact of quantum computing on encryption, it is essential to grasp the fundamental principles of quantum mechanics. Unlike classical computers, which use bits as the basic unit of information (0 or 1), quantum computers use quantum bits or qubits. Qubits can exist in numerous states simultaneously, due to the phenomenon of superposition. Additionally, qubits can be entangled, meaning the state of one qubit depends on the state of another, even if they are physically separated. These properties enable quantum computers
to perform specific calculations exponentially faster than classical computers.

The most prominent threat quantum computing poses to cybersecurity lies in Shor's algorithm, developed by mathematician Peter Shor in 1994. Shor's algorithm is designed to factor large numbers into their prime components efficiently. In classical computing, factoring large numbers with hundreds of digits is a highly time-consuming process, forming the basis of asymmetric encryption algorithms like RSA (Rivest–Shamir–Adleman). Nevertheless, Shor's algorithm can crack these encryption systems in polynomial time if it is run on a powerful enough quantum computer.

The implications of Shor's algorithm are profound. RSA encryption, widely used for securing communication and data, relies on the difficulty of factoring the product of two large prime numbers. With a quantum computer, this challenge becomes manageable, rendering RSA encryption and, consequently, many secure online transactions vulnerable to attacks. Similarly, other commonly used asymmetric encryption algorithms, such as ECC (Elliptic Curve Cryptography), are susceptible to quantum attacks.

While quantum computing poses a grave threat to asymmetric encryption, symmetric encryption algorithms and hash functions are less severely impacted. Symmetric encryption does not rely on mathematical issues such as factoring large numbers; instead, it uses a shared secret key for both encryption as well as decryption. Therefore, symmetric encryption remains resistant to quantum attacks, provided sufficiently long key lengths are used to withstand brute-force attempts.

Hash functions, which generate fixed-size outputs (hashes) from arbitrary-sized inputs, are also relatively resilient to quantum attacks. While Grover's algorithm, another quantum algorithm, can speed up the search for preimages of hash functions quadratically, it still requires a substantial quantum computer to pose a significant threat.

Recognizing the vulnerability of existing encryption methods to quantum attacks, the field of post-quantum cryptography has emerged. Post-quantum cryptography seeks to develop encryption algorithms and cryptographic techniques resistant to quantum attacks and can replace current cryptographic standards.

One approach in post-quantum cryptography is lattice-based cryptography. The encryption techniques that are thought to be resistant to quantum attacks are based on lattice problems. Lattice-based cryptography includes algorithms like NTRUEncrypt and Ring Learning With Errors (Ring-LWE), which are considered candidates for post-quantum encryption.

Another approach is code-based cryptography, which relies on the hardness of decoding randomly generated linear codes. Within the post-quantum cryptography community, the McEliece cryptosystem has garnered interest as an example of code-based cryptography.

Another area of study is hash-based cryptography. It is thought that hash-based signatures, like the Merkle signature scheme, are resistant to quantum attacks. These schemes are based on the concept of a one-way function, where it is easy to compute the hash but computationally infeasible to reverse it.

Additionally, multivariate polynomial and hash-based cryptography are being explored as potential candidates for post-quantum encryption. These cryptographic approaches introduce diversity into the field, ensuring multiple alternatives are available for securing digital communication in a post-quantum era.

While the development of post-quantum encryption methods is ongoing, organizations and governments are preparing for the quantum computing era by transitioning to quantum-safe cryptography. This transition involves assessing current cryptographic systems, identifying vulnerabilities, and gradually replacing them with quantum-resistant alternatives.

NIST, or known as National Institute of Standards and Technology, is leading the effort to standardize post-quantum cryptography. NIST initiated a public competition to evaluate and select quantum-resistant algorithms to serve as the foundation for future cryptographic standards. This process involves extensive peer review and scrutiny to ensure the chosen algorithms are robust against quantum attacks.

In addition to post-quantum cryptography, Quantum Key Distribution (QKD) is a quantum technology that offers a unique approach to securing communications. QKD leverages the principles of quantum mechanics to enable two parties to exchange cryptographic keys with the guarantee that any eavesdropping attempts would be detected. This level of security is based on the principle that quantum measurements inherently disturb the quantum state being measured, making it impossible for an eavesdropper to intercept the key without detection.

QKD is considered a highly secure method for key exchange, but it is still in its early stages of adoption due to practical challenges, such as the limited distance over which quantum keys can be transmitted and the need for specialized hardware.

In conclusion, the advent of quantum computing presents both opportunities and challenges for cybersecurity. Shor's algorithm threatens the security of widely used asymmetric encryption methods, necessitating the development and adoption of post-quantum cryptography. The transition to quantum-safe cryptography is underway, with organizations and governments actively preparing for the era of quantum computing. Quantum Key Distribution offers a promising alternative for securing communications, albeit with practical limitations.

As quantum computing technology advances, the cybersecurity community must remain vigilant, proactive, and adaptable. Quantum-resistant encryption methods and ongoing research and collaboration will ensure that our digital world remains secure in the face of this transformative technological shift. Integrating quantum-safe cryptography and developing innovative security solutions will ultimately determine our ability to safeguard sensitive information and maintain trust in the digital age.

CHAPTER XV

Building a Career in Cybersecurity

Career paths in cybersecurity

Given the value of data and the constantly changing character of cyber threats in the digital era, cybersecurity has appeared as one of the most important and dynamic subsectors of the technology industry. Because cyberattacks are becoming more frequent and sophisticated, businesses all over the world are in desperate need of qualified experts who can protect their digital assets. This has given rise to diverse career opportunities within the realm of cybersecurity, catering to a wide range of skills and interests. In this section, we will explore various career paths in cybersecurity, shedding light on the roles, responsibilities, and qualifications required for each.

Security analysts are the frontline defenders in the world of cybersecurity. They monitor an organization's network and systems for suspicious activities, investigate security incidents, and implement security measures to protect against threats. Strong analytical abilities and an in-depth comprehension of security technology and network protocols are prerequisites for security analysts. Entry-level positions are common for security analysts, who progress in their careers through experience and credentials such as CompTIA Security+ or Certified Information Systems Security Professional (CISSP).

In order to find flaws and vulnerabilities in an organization's systems, ethical hackers—also referred to as penetration testers or white-hat hackers—simulate cyberattacks. They perform controlled attacks with the organization's permission to help identify and address security flaws. Ethical hackers must think like malicious hackers to uncover potential risks. Certifications like Certified Ethical Hacker (CEH) and Offensive Security Certified Professional (OSCP) are highly regarded in this field.

Security architects design and build secure systems and networks. They work closely with other IT professionals to develop security solutions that meet an organization's specific needs. Security architects need a deep understanding of security technologies, best practices, and compliance requirements. Professionals in this field frequently work toward certifications like Certified Information Security Manager, abbreviated as CISM or Certified Information Systems Security Professional, abbreviated as CISSP.

Security consultants are employed by organizations to evaluate their security posture, pinpoint weaknesses, and suggest enhancements. They frequently work as independent contractors or for consulting firms. Strong project management and communication abilities are essential for a security consultant because they will be communicating intricate technical findings to stakeholders who are not technical. The Certified Information Systems Security Professional, abbreviated as CISSP and Certified Information Systems Auditor, abbreviated as CISA are two pertinent qualifications.

Security engineers focus on implementing and managing security solutions within an organization. They are responsible for configuring firewalls, intrusion detection systems, and other security tools and monitoring their effectiveness. Security engineers require a solid understanding of network and system administration, as well as security technologies. Certifications like Certified Information Systems Security Professional (or CISSP) or Certified Information Systems Security Professional (CompTIA Security+) are familiar in this field.

The Chief Information Security Officer, abbreviated as CISO, is a senior-level executive responsible for an organization's overall cybersecurity strategy and management. CISOs are crucial in defining cybersecurity policies, ensuring compliance with regulations, and managing security teams. To reach this level, professionals typically need extensive experience in cybersecurity, leadership skills, and often an advanced degree. Certifications like CISSP or CISM can be beneficial.

Security Operations Center (SOC) analysts work in a Security Operations Center, continuously monitoring an organization's security alerts and incidents. They investigate and respond to security events, ensuring that threats are detected and mitigated promptly. Over time, SOC analysts may start in entry-level positions and advance to more specialized roles, such as SOC manager or incident responder.

Forensic analysts specialize in collecting and analyzing digital evidence to investigate cybercrimes. They may work with law enforcement agencies, private investigators, or within organizations to uncover the details of a security incident. A strong background in digital forensics and knowledge of legal procedures are essential for this role.

Professionals in this field focus on educating employees and stakeholders about cybersecurity best practices. They develop training programs, conduct awareness campaigns, and create materials to help individuals understand and mitigate security risks. Effective communication skills and an in-depth comprehension of cybersecurity concepts are essential.

This career path involves researching to develop new cybersecurity technologies, tools, and strategies. Researchers often work for universities, government agencies, or private companies, contributing to advancements in cybersecurity. This role demands strong analytical and problem-solving skills and a deep knowledge of cybersecurity concepts and emerging threats.

Incident responders are in-charge of managing and mitigating security incidents when they occur. They work quickly to contain and remediate threats, minimizing damage and downtime. This role requires a rapid response to emerging threats and strong analytical skills to investigate incidents thoroughly.

Compliance and risk management professionals ensure that organizations adhere to cybersecurity regulations and standards. They assess risks, develop policies and procedures, and oversee compliance efforts. Certifications like Certified in Risk and Information Systems Control (or CRISC) and Certified Information Systems Auditor, abbreviated as CISA are valuable in this field.

In conclusion, the field of cybersecurity offers a wide array of career paths, each catering to different skills, interests, and expertise levels. Whether you're interested in analyzing security threats, designing secure systems, or managing security policies, you have a cybersecurity role. Continuous learning and certifications are key to advancing in this dynamic field, as staying up-to-date with the latest threats and technologies is crucial to effectively protecting digital assets in an increasingly connected world. With the ever-growing demand for cybersecurity professionals, a rewarding and impactful career in this field awaits those dedicated to securing the digital landscape.

Certifications and training for cybersecurity professionals

Staying ahead of threats and guaranteeing the security of digital assets has become a primary issue for enterprises globally in the constantly changing field of cybersecurity. Cybersecurity professionals must develop a wide range of abilities and knowledge to meet this demand. These workers need certifications and training programs to give them the knowledge and skills needed to protect networks, systems, and data.

The importance of certifications and training in cybersecurity cannot be overstated. Cybersecurity is a multifaceted domain, covering various aspects such as network security, cloud security, ethical hacking, and compliance. As technology advances and cyber threats become increasingly sophisticated, professionals must continually update their skills and knowledge. Certifications and training programs offer structured and standardized ways to achieve this, ensuring cybersecurity professionals are well-equipped to address current and emerging challenges.

Certifications serve as a validation of an individual's expertise and skills in specific areas of cybersecurity.

Employers recognize them as a reliable indicator of a candidate's competence and commitment to the field. Additionally, certifications can enhance job prospects, leading to career advancement and higher earning potential.

Training programs complement certifications by providing in-depth knowledge, hands-on experience, and practical skills. These programs often include simulations and real-world scenarios, allowing professionals to apply their learning in a controlled environment. Training helps individuals prepare for certification exams and equips them with the practical skills required to excel in their roles.

In cybersecurity, a diverse range of certifications are available, each catering to different skills, interests, and career goals. Some of the most recognized and sought-after certifications include Certified Information Systems Security Professional, abbreviated as CISSP, Certified Ethical Hacker (CEH), Certified Information Security Manager (CISM), CompTIA Security+, and many more. These certifications cover a broad spectrum of topics, allowing professionals to specialize in areas that align with their interests and career aspirations.

Certifications play a crucial role in career advancement for cybersecurity professionals. They provide a clear path for individuals to progress from entry-level roles to more specialized and senior positions. For instance, CompTIA Security+ is often pursued by newcomers to the field, providing them with foundational knowledge and a competitive edge when entering the job market. As professionals gain experience and expertise, they can pursue intermediate and advanced certifications like CISSP or CISM, which open doors to leadership and managerial roles in cybersecurity.

Certified professionals are not only more likely to secure high-demand cybersecurity roles but also tend to earn higher salaries than their non-certified peers. Employers view certifications as proof of expertise, making certified professionals more valuable assets to their organizations. Certification holders are often rewarded with increased compensation, reflecting their commitment to ongoing learning and professional development.

Furthermore, certifications are not static achievements. Many certifications require ongoing professional development to maintain certification status. This encourages professionals to stay updated on the latest threats, technologies, and best practices, ensuring they remain at the forefront of the field. Continuing education is crucial in a domain where the threat landscape constantly evolves.

In conclusion, certifications and training programs are indispensable for cybersecurity professionals. They provide the knowledge, skills, and validation needed to excel in a field critical to digital asset security. With the vast array of certifications available, professionals can tailor their certification paths to align with their career goals and interests. Whether starting a career in cybersecurity, advancing to a leadership position, or specializing in a specific domain, certifications and ongoing training are the keys to success in this dynamic and ever-evolving field. Cybersecurity professionals are vital in safeguarding the digital world from evolving threats and vulnerabilities by continually investing in their education and skill development.

Tips for starting and advancing a cybersecurity career

One of the most important fields in today's technologically advanced society is cybersecurity. With the growing dependence of both individuals and businesses on digital technology, safeguarding confidential information and reducing cyber risks have become critical. As a result, positions related to cybersecurity are in great demand and present profitable prospects for individuals who possess the necessary abilities and mindset.

It's essential to have a solid foundation in computer science and information technology before pursuing a career in cybersecurity. A bachelor's degree in a related field, such as cybersecurity, information technology, or computer science, is a good place to start. A solid educational foundation will provide you with an in-depth comprehension of computer networks and systems as well as the necessary technical abilities.

Cybersecurity is a field that demands continuous learning and adaptability. Cyber threats are constantly evolving, and new technologies emerge regularly. Stay curious and committed to expanding your knowledge. Read books, research papers, and industry publications. Take online courses and attend conferences and workshops. Engage in hands-on labs and simulations to gain practical experience.

Technical proficiency is the cornerstone of a successful cybersecurity career. Familiarize yourself with operating systems (Windows, Linux, macOS), networking concepts, programming languages (Python, C, Java), and cybersecurity tools. Hands-on experience with configuring firewalls, intrusion detection systems, and penetration testing tools is invaluable.

Beyond technical skills, grasp fundamental cybersecurity concepts. Learn about encryption, authentication, access control, risk management, and incident response. A deep understanding of these principles will enable you to make informed decisions and design effective security measures.

Certifications are widely recognized in cybersecurity and can boost your career prospects. Consider certifications such as Certified Information Systems Security Professional, abbreviated as CISSP, Certified Ethical Hacker, abbreviated as CEH, Certified Information Security Manager (CISM), CompTIA Security+, and Certified Information Systems Auditor (CISA), among others. These certifications validate your expertise and commitment to the field.

Hands-on experience is invaluable in cybersecurity. Seek internships, entry-level positions, or volunteer opportunities to gain practical exposure to real-world scenarios. Working with security tools, analyzing logs, and participating in incident response activities will enhance your skills and make you more attractive to employers.

Soft skills are just as vital for a successful cybersecurity profession as technical expertise. In the field, critical thinking, problem-solving, collaboration, and communication abilities are highly valued. Cybersecurity experts frequently have to work well with cross-functional teams and explain difficult technical topics to stakeholders who are not technical.

In cybersecurity, a diverse range of certifications are available, each catering to different skills, interests, and career goals. Some of the most recognized and sought-after certifications include Certified Information Systems

Security Professional, abbreviated as CISSP, Certified Ethical Hacker, abbreviated as CEH, Certified Information Security Manager (CISM), CompTIA Security+, and many more. These certifications cover a broad spectrum of topics, allowing professionals to specialize in areas that align with their interests and career aspirations.

A key element of career advancement is networking. Attend cybersecurity conferences, join industry associations, and participate in online forums and communities. Building a professional network can lead to mentorship opportunities, job referrals, and knowledge sharing with peers.

To excel in cybersecurity, you must stay informed about current cyber threats and trends. Follow cybersecurity news, subscribe to threat intelligence feeds, and review security incident reports regularly. Understanding the threat landscape is essential for proactive defense.

Consider practicing ethical hacking or penetration testing to understand vulnerabilities and attack techniques better. Ethical hackers play a crucial role in identifying and mitigating security weaknesses. Pursuing certifications like Certified Ethical Hacker (CEH) can formalize this skill set.

For career advancement, consider pursuing a master's degree in cybersecurity or a related field. Advanced degrees can open doors to leadership positions and research opportunities. Additionally, explore advanced certifications such as Certified Information Systems Security Professional, abbreviated as CISSP, Certified Information Security Manager (CISM), or Offensive Security Certified Professional (OSCP) to demonstrate your expertise further.

Cybersecurity professionals often have access to sensitive information and systems. Embrace a robust code of ethics and prioritize integrity and confidentiality in your work. Upholding ethical standards is essential for maintaining trust in the field.

Cybersecurity is not without its challenges. The field can be demanding, requiring long hours, stress management, and the ability to adapt quickly to new threats. Be prepared for the continuous challenges and the need for resilience.

Consider giving back to the cybersecurity community. Mentor aspiring professionals, share your knowledge, and contribute to open-source projects or security research. Giving back helps others and enhances your reputation in the field.

In conclusion, a cybersecurity career offers immense opportunities for those willing to invest in their education, skills, and commitment to the field. Whether you're starting your journey or looking to advance, the key is continuously learning, adapting, and staying informed. Building technical expertise, pursuing certifications, developing soft skills, and embracing a strong code of ethics are all critical components of a successful cybersecurity career. As you navigate this dynamic field, remember that your contributions are vital in safeguarding the digital world from cyber threats and vulnerabilities.

CONCLUSION

Recap of key points

We've covered an extensive spectrum of topics in this series of sections on different facets of cybersecurity, from the foundations of network security to the significance of cloud security, ethical hacking, and incident response. Recapping the main ideas covered will clarify that cybersecurity is a broad and dynamic field that reflects the ever-changing digital reality.

Above all, the importance of cybersecurity cannot be emphasized enough. The preservation of vital infrastructure and the protection of sensitive data are crucial in a time when digital technologies power practically every element of contemporary life. An evolving threat landscape requires vigilance from both individuals and organizations.

It is essential to comprehend the fundamentals of network security. Implementing firewalls, intrusion detection systems, and encryption is just one aspect of effective network security; other aspects include vulnerability management and identification. Identifying gaps in systems and networks is made possible by vulnerability scanning and assessment technologies, which enable businesses to take proactive measures to mitigate potential security concerns.

Moreover, penetration testing—a critical procedure in which ethical hackers mimic actual attacks to evaluate an organization's security posture—is included in the proactive strategy. An organization can strengthen its defenses by using different types of penetration testing, like the Black Box, White Box, and Grey Box, which provide varied degrees of insight into its weaknesses.

Organizations need to implement holistic approaches to vulnerability management, including risk assessment, patch management, and prioritization. Because vulnerabilities are dynamic, continuously monitoring and adjusting is necessary to stay one step ahead of possible threats.

Because attackers frequently target them, web applications require strong security measures. If left unchecked, common online application vulnerabilities like SQL injection, cross-site scripting (XSS), and CSRF attacks can have disastrous results. To reduce these risks, it is imperative to utilize secure web application best practices, including code review, input validation, and session management.

Furthermore, it is impossible to exaggerate the importance of cloud security. Network security is becoming increasingly significant as more businesses use cloud services. Sensitive data is kept safe in cloud environments by putting best practices for cloud security, such as identity and access management (or IAM), encryption, and monitoring, into practice.

Given the widespread utilization of smartphones and mobile apps, mobile device security and mobile app security are also essential factors to consider. Bring Your Own Device (BYOD) guidelines offer cybersecurity opportunities and challenges. They can boost output and flexibility, but they also bring with them security threats that need to be properly handled.

Social engineering attacks, including phishing and pretexting, take advantage of psychological traits in people to trick them into disclosing private information or taking activities that put their security at risk. The best defenses against these deceptive strategies are awareness campaigns and training initiatives.

In cybersecurity, firms should take a proactive stance by getting ready for incidents. Planning and carrying out incident response plans are crucial to reducing the effects of security breaches when they happen. Disaster recovery plans guarantee business continuation in the event of unanticipated disasters, complementing incident response.

Respecting the laws and rules governing cybersecurity operations is crucial because of the potential legal ramifications of hacking and the ethical issues that ethical hackers must address. In addition to avoiding legal ramifications, remaining ethically and legally compliant upholds integrity and confidence in the industry.

Finally, we looked at the trends in cybersecurity that are happening now and in the future, like how machine learning and artificial intelligence are becoming more and more critical in threat identification and mitigation. Despite its potential, quantum computing presents difficulties for encryption and necessitates advancements in cryptography methods.

In conclusion, the field of cybersecurity is dynamic and complex, necessitating ongoing education and adjustment. To safeguard digital assets and preserve the integrity of the digital world, being knowledgeable and proactive is crucial in matters ranging from network security to cloud security, ethical hacking to incident response. Professionals in cybersecurity are essential to protecting our globalized society, and their knowledge and commitment to combating cyberattacks are invaluable.

The ongoing importance of cybersecurity and ethical hacking

The significance of ethical hacking and cybersecurity is only increasing in today's ever-more digital society. Protecting sensitive data and systems against cyber threats is crucial as technology becomes increasingly ingrained in our daily lives and businesses depend on digital infrastructure to run. This section examines the ongoing importance of ethical hacking and cybersecurity, highlighting its function in safeguarding digital assets and upholding people's and organizations' confidence.

The methods and strategies used by cybercriminals are always changing along with the digital landscape. Threat actors can be anything from lone hackers looking to make money to highly skilled state-sponsored organizations with malevolent intentions. Cyberattacks may target financial resources, key infrastructure, private data, or even national security. As a result, companies need to be on the lookout for new threats and modify their cybersecurity protocols accordingly.

The first line of defense against data breaches, which can have serious repercussions for people and organizations alike, is cybersecurity. Loss of privacy, financial fraud, and identity theft are all possible outcomes of compromised personal data. Data breaches cause financial losses, harm to a company's brand, and sometimes even legal repercussions. Cybersecurity practices, such as access control, encryption, and routine vulnerability assessments, are crucial for preventing sensitive information from getting into the wrong hands.

One of the most important functions of ethical hacking, sometimes called penetration testing or white-hat hacking, is to find vulnerabilities before malevolent hackers may take use of them. With the owner's permission, ethical hackers utilize their expertise to mimic cyberattacks on networks, systems, and applications. By being proactive, organizations may find and fix vulnerabilities, which lowers the likelihood that successful attacks will occur.

Experts in their field, ethical hackers possess the same mindset as cybercriminals but apply their knowledge for the benefit of society. They identify gaps in security measures, draw attention to possible dangers, and suggest countermeasures. Ethical hackers offer priceless insights that can significantly improve an organization's security posture.

Another factor highlighting the significance of cybersecurity is the expanding set of rules and compliance requirements. Governments and trade associations are placing more and more legal obligations on businesses to safeguard confidential information and keep up-to-date cybersecurity safeguards. Serious fines and harm to one's reputation may arise from breaking these rules. As a result, businesses are investing in cybersecurity to both comply with regulations and for security's sake.

Even though technology plays a big role in cybersecurity, individuals are still one of the most important components. Social engineering assaults, including phishing and pretexting, use psychological techniques to trick people into divulging private information or acting in a way that could be detrimental. The best defense against these strategies are effective cybersecurity awareness and training initiatives. A continual endeavor to guarantee that people stay alert in the face of changing threats is educating staff members and individuals about the risks and best practices.

The cybersecurity field has opportunities and difficulties in store for the future. Machine learning along with artificial intelligence are becoming increasingly crucial for identifying and reducing threats. AI-powered solutions can evaluate enormous datasets in real-time to spot irregularities and possible threats, enabling businesses to react skillfully to cyberattacks.

However, the development of quantum computing presents a serious threat to encryption. The development of quantum-resistant cryptography is required since existing encryption algorithms could be broken by quantum computers. Innovation and adaptation are required for the cybersecurity community to remain ahead of this new danger.

In conclusion, it is impossible to exaggerate the continued significance of ethical hacking and cybersecurity. As the digital terrain changes, so do the potential threats it poses. In addition to being crucial for maintaining individual privacy, safeguarding sensitive data, adhering to laws, and thwarting cyberattacks are also critical for maintaining the security and stability of nations and organizations.

As a preventative measure against cyberattacks, ethical hacking assists companies in locating and fixing security holes before malevolent actors may take advantage of them. The continuous fight to secure digital assets depends heavily on cooperation between cybersecurity experts and ethical hackers.

With new technologies like AI and quantum computing changing the game, the field of cybersecurity faces both opportunities and difficulties in the future. Collaboration, constant learning, and adaptation are going to be crucial for cybersecurity experts and ethical hackers to traverse this rapidly evolving industry effectively. Ultimately, their knowledge and commitment are critical to maintaining the safety and integrity of the digital world.

Encouragement for readers to continue learning

In the dynamic and constantly changing fields of cybersecurity and ethical hacking, acquiring new information and abilities is recommended and necessary. The need of safeguarding private data, vital infrastructure, and sensitive information cannot be emphasized in a society where digital technologies are used extensively. As a result, adopting a lifelong learning mindset is crucial for all aspirant and seasoned professionals in this field. This section urges readers to pursue further knowledge in ethical hacking and cybersecurity while also acting as a helpful reminder.

The continually changing threat landscape is one of the main reasons to keep learning about cybersecurity. Cybercriminals are never-ending in their search for fresh points of weakness and avenues for attack. A stagnant level of knowledge could result in data breaches, the exploitation of vulnerabilities, and serious harm to both individuals and businesses. By constantly studying, you can stay on top of the most recent threats and create proactive defenses.

In the field of cybersecurity, the quick development of new technology presents both benefits and difficulties. A few technological developments that greatly impact cybersecurity are cloud computing, quantum computing, artificial intelligence, and the Internet of Things (IoT). Being aware of these technologies and how security interacts with them is essential to fighting off potential attacks.

Within the cybersecurity domain, one's professional value increases with more knowledge. Continually learning new things improves your effectiveness in protecting systems and data and creates opportunities for professional growth. Professionals that are committed to remaining up to date in this quickly evolving field are highly valued by employers and may lead to improved career prospects and higher earning potential.

One essential element of cybersecurity is ethical hacking, sometimes called penetration testing or white-hat hacking. Before malevolent hackers may take advantage of vulnerabilities and flaws in systems, networks, and applications, ethical hackers utilize their expertise to find and fix them. By adopting ethical hacking and developing your expertise in this field, you help organizations safeguard sensitive data and secure their digital assets, which benefits society as a whole.

Professionals in cybersecurity are crucial to maintaining privacy, national security, and vital infrastructure. When it comes to defending against cyberthreats that can ruin lives and economies, your experience can really help. One of the most potent incentives to keep learning and developing in your cybersecurity profession is the knowledge that your work makes the internet safer.

The community surrounding ethical hacking and cybersecurity is large and friendly. Regardless of your level of experience, there are many of chances to interact with colleagues, mentors, and industry professionals.

There are networking, learning, and knowledge sharing venues, including local meetups, webinars, seminars, and online forums. Participating in this group can offer motivation, direction, and a feeling of acceptance.

You can't take your accomplishments in the fields of ethical hacking and cybersecurity for granted. Rather, they signify an enduring education path, flexibility, and commitment. Accept the excitement of exploration, the difficulty of figuring out challenging problems, and the fulfillment that comes from knowing that you're making the internet safer.

In conclusion, it is critical to stress the value of ongoing education in ethical hacking and cybersecurity. Because of the dynamic nature of threats, the emergence of new technologies, and the increasing importance of digital security, it's critical to maintain curiosity, take initiative, and commit to learning new things. In addition to helping your career, your commitment is essential to making sure that everyone has access to digital technology in the future. Thus, I encourage you to continue studying, developing, and having a good influence in the field of ethical hacking and cybersecurity.

Thank you for buying and reading/ listening to our book. If you found this book useful/ helpful please take a few minutes and leave a review on the platform where you purchased our book. Your feedback matters greatly to us.